Wendy Williams • Jean Sasso

English as a Second Language   **Elementary Cycle Three**

STUDENT BOOK B

CEC

LES ÉDITIONS CEC INC.

8101, boul. Métropolitain Est, Anjou, Qc, Canada H1J 1J9
Téléphone : (514) 351-6010 Télécopieur : (514) 351-3534

Managing Director, ESL
Julie Hough

Production Manager
Danielle Latendresse

Project Editor
Michèle Devlin

Cover and page design
Matteau Parent graphisme et communication inc.
Geneviève Guérard, designer

Illustrations
Paule Thibault
Sébastien Gagnon

Dépôt légal,
Bibliothèque nationale du Québec,
2ᵉ trimestre 2003

Legal deposit,
National Library of Canada,
2nd quarter 2003

ISBN 2-7617-1933-6
Printed in Canada

1 2 3 4 5 6 08 07 06 05 04 03

About the Authors

Wendy Williams has been teaching English as a second language for over 25 years in Chicoutimi (Ville de Saguenay). She wrote teaching materials at the elementary level for her colleagues before joining the CEC team as co-author of the All-Star series of activity books and of *Clues to English* for Grade 6 students. Wendy is also co-author of *The New Clues to English, Book A*.

Jean Sasso was co-author of *Clues to English* for Grades 4 and 6 and the All-Star series of activity books. Some of her work was retained for *The New Keys to English, Book B*. After a long career teaching ESL, Jean is currently enjoying retirement.

Acknowledgements

The authors wish to express their thanks to the whole team at CEC for their steadfast commitment to this series and their role in bringing the material to fruition. Heartfelt thanks go to Julie Hough for her direction and leadership, and to Leena M. Sandblom for her constant support on the whole project, to Michèle Devlin for her excellent editorial work and unfailing good humour, and to the people at Matteau Parent for their fine graphic work.

They also wish to thank the participants of the focus groups and follow-up consultations for their invaluable advice. Their insights helped to make *The New Keys to English* what it is today.

Special thanks go to Camil for his constant support, patience and love. Special thanks also to Hélène Saucier, a cherished friend and wonderful teacher.

Sources

Pages 16-17: Text adapted from *The Pizza Book* by Stephen Krensky; text copyright © 1992 by Stephen Krensky. **Pages 34-35:** Photo of Marc Gagnon © Michel PONOMAREFF / PONOPRESSE. Photo of Craig Kielburger © Atlan / PDV Images Monde / Point de Vue / Gamma / PONOPRESSE. Photo of Gizmo by Judi Azula © 2003 Helping Hands. **Page 36:** Illustration of Captain Canuck © 2002 Richard Comely. Photo of Terry Fox © Gail Harvey, courtesy of the Terry Fox Foundation. Photo of hockey stick © PhotoDisc. Photo of table setting © Creativ Collection. **Page 37:** Photo of Jamie Salé © Deseret News / Gamma / PONOPRESSE. **Page 58:** Photo of Alexander Graham Bell © Topham / PONOPRESSE. **Pages 59 and 62:** Text of "Important Numbers" and "Emergency Mystery" adapted from *The Phone Book: Instant Communication from Smoke Signals to Satellites and Beyond* by Elizabeth McLeod; text copyright © 1995 by Elizabeth MacLeod; reprinted by permission of Kids Can Press Ltd. **Page 89:** Photos of the 2001-2002 Third Cycle class at École Ste-Claire courtesy of Wendy Williams. **Page 104:** Photos of watch and teddy bear © Creativ Collection. Photos of starfish, kitten, ball and ribbon © PhotoDisc. **Page 106:** Photo of boy courtesy of Gabriel Boucher. Photo of girl © PhotoDisc. **Pages 120-121:** Photo of girl © UNICEF / 92-023 / J. Isaac. Photo of classroom © UNICEF / Pirozzi / Zambia. Photos of globe and slate © Creativ Collection. **Page 123:** Photo courtesy of Wendy Williams. **Page 132:** Photo of dictionary and copybooks © Artville. **Page 137:** Photo of orange © Artville. **Page 139:** Photo of clock © PhotoDisc. Photo of pancakes © Artville. **Page 143:** photo of television © PhotoDisc.

Contents

Help Station

Keys characters

 Michael

 Jenny

 Enrico

 Melissa

Keys logos

 Strategy

 Listening activity

 Writing activity

 Grammar

 Pair activity

 Team activity

 Class activity

 Major practice

Instructions

What's your brother's name?

David.

ask **answer**

find

read

share

think

use

write

Fundamentals

How do you say *souris* in English?
How do you spell *mouse*?

1 **Making connections**

A Look at the categories on the lines around the star. What is your favourite for each category?

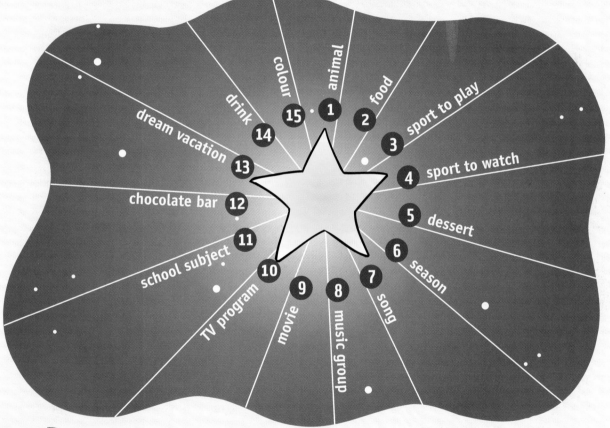

colour
animal
drink
food
dream vacation
sport to play
sport to watch
chocolate bar
dessert
school subject
season
TV program
movie
music group
song

15 1 14 2 13 3 12 4 11 5 10 6 9 7 8

B Connect with your classmates.
Find a classmate with the same favourites.
Look at the key language for help.

C Report to the class.

KEY LANGUAGE

I have a connection with Jenny. **Our** favourite dessert is chocolate cake.

lookahead

five   5

TALK

2 Strategy station

Strategies help you learn.
Look at the classroom activities.
What strategies can help you in each activity?
Look at the next page for ideas.

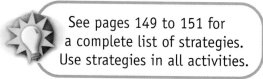
See pages 149 to 151 for a complete list of strategies. Use strategies in all activities.

CLASSROOM ACTIVITIES

1 playing a game

2 learning new words

3 interviewing a classmate

4 writing a text

5 listening to the teacher

6 reading a story

7 singing a song

8 watching a video

9 making a collage

10 working on the computer

STRATEGIES

❸ School stuff

These are people and things you see at school.

A Identify the pictures.
Spell the words.

B Decide what words are for...

• people in a school

• objects in a classroom

• places in a school

• things in a backpack

4 Number jumble

A Play Higher – Lower.

> **How to play**
> - One person chooses a number and writes it down.
> - The other players try to guess the number.
>   The clues are HIGHER (↑) and LOWER (↓).
> - Listen carefully.

🔑 KEY LANGUAGE

- Is it 31? / No, lower.
- Is it 10? / No, higher.
- Is it 20? / No, higher.
- Is it 22? / Yes, that's it. Good for you!

B Do some mathemagic. Try these math tricks.
Your teacher can predict your answers.

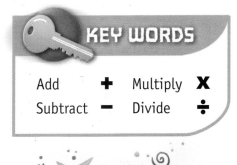

🔑 KEY WORDS

Add	**+**	Multiply **✕**
Subtract	**−**	Divide **÷**

Choose any number.
- Add 5.
- Multiply by 3.
- Subtract 9.
- Divide by 3.
- Subtract your original number.

Choose any number.
- Add 7.
- Multiply by 2.
- Subtract 4.
- Divide by 2.
- Subtract your original number.

⑤ All about Me

This activity includes pictures and writing.

Here is the front of Jenny's *All about Me*.   **Here is the back.**

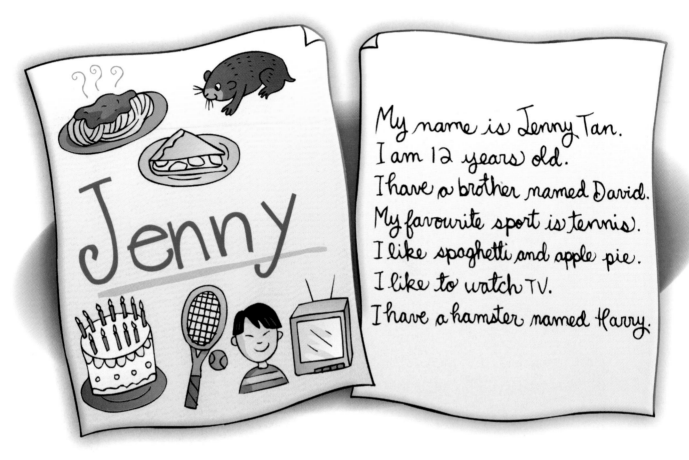

My name is Jenny Tan.
I am 12 years old.
I have a brother named David.
My favourite sport is tennis.
I like spaghetti and apple pie.
I like to watch TV.
I have a hamster named Harry.

A Look at Jenny's pictures.
1. Which one do you prefer?
2. What foods does she like?
3. What is her favourite sport?
4. Does she have a sister?

Read her text.
5. Find the sentences about
   • Jenny's age
   • a pet and a family member
   • Jenny's preferences

B Write your composition. Your teacher will give you instructions and a checklist.

GET HELP

models   **a dictionary**   **my teacher**   **a checklist**

6 Class reporters

A Show your *All about Me* creation to your classmates and explain it. Listen to others and take notes.

KEY LANGUAGE

B Use your notes to write reports. Refer to the Grammar Power capsule for help.

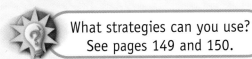

What strategies can you use? See pages 149 and 150.

GRAMMAR POWER — Pronouns and possessives

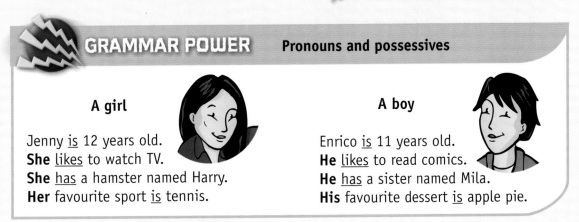

A girl

Jenny is 12 years old.
She likes to watch TV.
She has a hamster named Harry.
Her favourite sport is tennis.

A boy

Enrico is 11 years old.
He likes to read comics.
He has a sister named Mila.
His favourite dessert is apple pie.

⑦ Backpacks

A FACTS

Backpacks are popular with students from kindergarten to university.
But heavy backpacks can sometimes cause back pain.
Here are some ideas to prevent this problem.

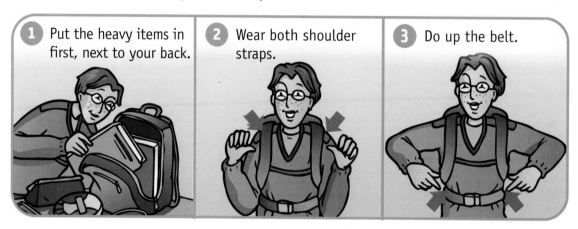

1 Put the heavy items in first, next to your back.

2 Wear both shoulder straps.

3 Do up the belt.

Do you have any other ideas?

B FUN

Play the Backpack game.

People Bingo

A Match the questions and the pictures.

KEY LANGUAGE

1 When is your birthday?

2 What's your phone number?

3 Where do you live?

4 What's your mom's/dad's name?

5 Do you have any brothers/sisters?

6 Do you have any pets?

Look at questions 1 to 6.
- What questions have **Yes** or **No** as answers?
- What question word asks about time or a date?
- What question word asks about a place?

B Write down your personal information.

C Ask your classmates the questions. Write down their answers.

D Play People Bingo. Have fun!

Bingo!

LOOKback

UNIT 1 Pizza!

A Pizza is a popular food.
Give some reasons why.
Look at the pictures for ideas.

A

B

C

D

1

2

3

B What can you put on a pizza?
- Match the pictures with the key words.
- Practice the key words with a partner.
- Make a list of other pizza words with your teacher.

What strategies can you use in this activity? See pages 150 and 151.

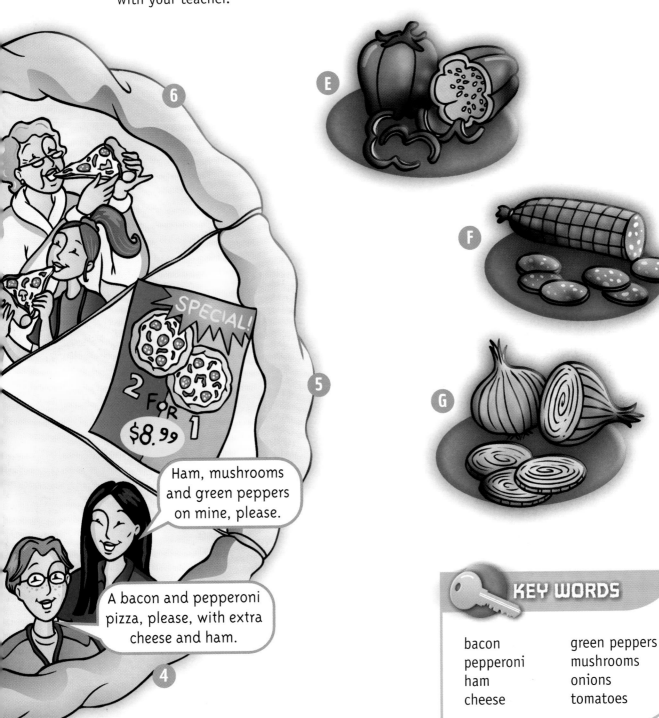

E

F

G

6

5

SPECIAL!

2 FOR 1

$8.99

Ham, mushrooms and green peppers on mine, please.

A bacon and pepperoni pizza, please, with extra cheese and ham.

4

KEY WORDS

bacon	green peppers
pepperoni	mushrooms
ham	onions
cheese	tomatoes

C What are your pizza-eating habits?
Your teacher has some questions for you.

1 The history of pizza

BEFORE READING

What strategies can you use in this activity? See pages 150 and 151.

Look at the pictures.

1 Is pizza a new food?

2 Is the tomato originally from North America or Europe?

3 Where was the modern pizza invented?

Look at the text.

4 Find English words that resemble French words.

The first pizzas were just crusts with oil and some herbs on top. That was 2000 years ago, in ancient Rome.

When European explorers came to America, they discovered tomatoes.

In the 1700s, Italian chefs used tomatoes to make a sauce for pizza.

KEY WORDS

crust

topping
ingredient you put
on top of food

oil

flag

The modern pizza was invented in 1889 by the famous chef Raffaele Esposito. He created a special pizza in honour of Queen Margherita of Italy. He added a new topping – mozzarella cheese. The white cheese, red tomato sauce and green herbs matched the colours of the Italian flag. The queen loved the new pizza, which was named in her honour, pizza *alla* Margherita.

Today, people all over the world like to eat pizza. There are many different kinds of pizza. Vegetarian pizza, sausage pizza and Hawaiian pizza are very popular. What's your favourite?

AFTER READING

1 What did you learn about pizza?
Your teacher has some questions for you.

2 Complete the Pizza Timeline. Your teacher will explain.

A   B   C   D

2 Favourite pizzas

A Think about your favourite toppings.
Ask your teammates what they like on their pizzas.
Look at the key language for help.
Record their answers and add up the totals.

B Tell other teams about your results.
Listen to other teams and write down their results.

> What strategies can you use in this activity? See pages 150 and 151.

KEY LANGUAGE

What do you like on your pizza?

Just pepperoni and cheese.

I like ham, cheese and mushrooms. What about you?

That's 4 for cheese, right?

Right.

Everybody likes cheese.
Two students like green peppers.
One person likes mushrooms.
Nobody likes onions.

Everybody likes bacon and pepperoni.
One person prefers ham and one person likes tomatoes.

C Calculate the class totals.
- What toppings are the most popular?
- What toppings does nobody like?
- What can you put on a pizza for the entire class?

③ Personal pizzas

> My pizza is pizza
> alla Melissa. It
> has tomato sauce,
> cheese and double
> pepperoni.
> It's great!

> My pizza is the best.
> Pizza *al* Michael has
> tomato sauce, double
> cheese, bacon, pepperoni
> and ham.

A 1. Read Melissa's and Michael's texts. Which pizza do you prefer?
   2. Find two expressions that mean these pizzas are very good.
   3. What Italian word is used to name pizza for a girl? For a boy?
   4. What sentences describe the ingredients? Identify the verb.
   5. What punctuation separates the words in the list of ingredients?

B Write your composition.
Your teacher will give you
instructions and a checklist.

GRAMMAR POWER

To review punctuation, see page 139.

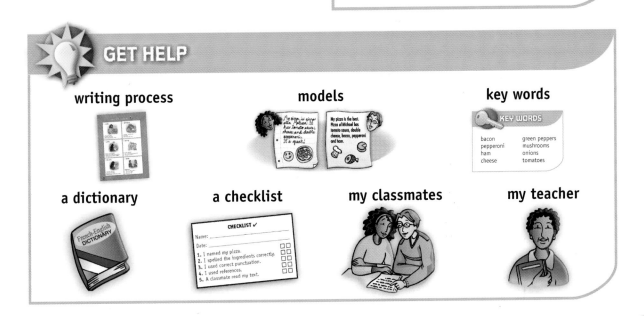

💡 **GET HELP**

writing process

models

key words

KEY WORDS

bacon	green peppers
pepperoni	mushrooms
ham	onions
cheese	tomatoes

a dictionary

French-English DICTIONARY

a checklist

CHECKLIST ✔
Name:
Date:
1. I named my pizza.
2. I spelled the ingredients correctly.
3. I used correct punctuation.
4. I used references.
5. A classmate read my text.

my classmates

my teacher

4 Eating out

A Look at the menu. What would you like to order?

The Pizza Palace

PIZZAS	SMALL	MEDIUM	LARGE
Solo tomato sauce and cheese	$6.25	$7.25	$8.50
Duo tomato sauce, cheese, mushrooms and pepperoni	$7.25	$8.25	$9.50
Super trio tomato sauce, cheese, bacon, salami and pepperoni	$8.25	$9.25	$10.50
Special tomato sauce, cheese, green peppers and bacon	$7.50	$8.50	$9.75
Vegetarian tomato sauce, cheese, green peppers, tomatoes and mushrooms	$7.75	$8.75	$10.00
Hawaiian cheese, pineapple and ham	$8.25	$9.25	$10.50

Add **$1.50** for double cheese.   Add **$1.50** for each additional topping.   Home delivery **$2.00**

DRINKS

Soft drinks	
small	$2.00
medium	$2.50
large	$3.00
Milkshakes	
vanilla, chocolate	$2.50
Tea, coffee	$2.50

DESSERTS

Ice cream	$3.00
Chocolate cake	$3.50
Apple or sugar pie	$3.75

B Use the key language on page 21 to practice ordering.

KEY LANGUAGE

The **SERVER** says:

The **CUSTOMER** says:

Are you ready to order?

Yes, I'd like to order a pizza, please.

What do you want on your pizza?

I want bacon and mushrooms, please.

What do you want to drink?

A milkshake, please.

Do you want a dessert?

Yes. I'll have chocolate cake, please.

5 Ordering a pizza

BEFORE LISTENING

1 What is Michael doing?
2 Do you know how to order a pizza by phone?
3 What information is necessary?

Hello. The Pizza Palace. Can I help you?

Yes. I'd like to order a pizza, please.

AFTER LISTENING

Work with a partner.
1 Fill out an order for yourself.
2 Take your partner's order.

⑥ FUN FACTS

A Read the questions. Think about possible answers.

What strategies can you use in this activity?

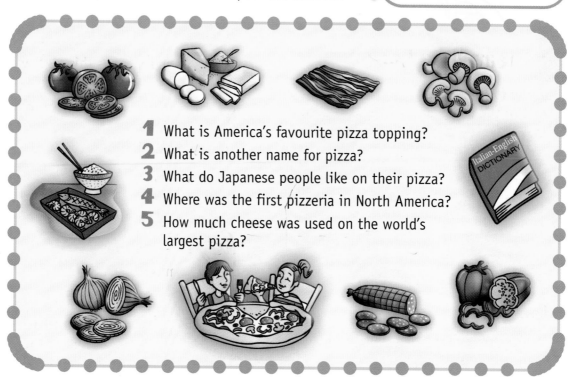

1 What is America's favourite pizza topping?
2 What is another name for pizza?
3 What do Japanese people like on their pizza?
4 Where was the first pizzeria in North America?
5 How much cheese was used on the world's largest pizza?

B Your teacher will give you an answer sheet.

• Discuss the choices with your teammates.
• Choose an answer for each question.
• Mark your score.

FUN FACTS RATING	
4 - 5	You are a pizza star.
2 - 3	You are a pizza expert.
0 - 1	Have pizza for supper.

The Great Pizza Race

Get ready for the game.
- Practice the words on the menu on page 20.
- Review the key language in this unit.
- Look in the reference section for other language to help you play this game.

Your teacher will give you a game board and move cards. Have fun!

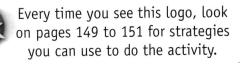
Every time you see this logo, look on pages 149 to 151 for strategies you can use to do the activity.

It's my turn. I'd like mushrooms on my pizza, please.

Mmm. I like mushrooms too.

Way to go, Enrico! Your turn, Jenny.

A Story

GET READY

1 **Take a look.**
- Who is in this story?
- Where does this story take place?
- When does the story happen?

2 **Use what you know.**
- How do you make pizza?
- How do you prepare for a party?

3 **Make a prediction.**
- Read the title of this story.
  What trouble do you think Andy has in the story?

4 **Learn the key words.**

KEY WORDS

throw	freezer	jar	lots a big quantity

turn on			
turn off	dial	scream	together
oven			

DOUBLE TROUBLE

1

It's Friday after school, the best time of the week. Andy is excited because his friends are coming to his house for a party. He throws his backpack under the bed and starts to prepare for the party.

2

He goes to the kitchen to make sure there are lots of chips and soft drinks. But he decides he wants to make something special for his friends.

3

Mrs. Kennedy is getting ready to leave.

Mom, is it OK if I make a pizza for my party?

No problem, Mom. I've watched you make pizza lots of times.

Sure, but I can't help you. I have to pick up your sister at her judo class. The pizza crust is in the freezer. Make sure you read the directions. And please clean up when you're finished.

4

Andy reads the directions for making one pizza. His friends love pizza, so he decides to make two. He assembles all the toppings: mushrooms, green peppers, tomato sauce, cheese and pepperoni.

Hmm...two pizzas, that's two jars of tomato sauce, two green peppers, double the cheese and mushrooms too. Oh yeah, and lots of pepperoni.

5

Andy cuts up the green peppers and mushrooms. He puts all the toppings on the two pizzas.

6

Next, he turns on the oven.

Well, I doubled all the toppings to make two pizzas. I suppose it's a good idea to double the temperature too. Two times 375° is 750°. But that number isn't even on the dial. I'll just set it at 500° and double the time to 50 minutes.

7

Andy puts the two pizzas in the oven. They look fantastic.

8

Next, Andy goes downstairs to choose some CDs for the party. He closes the basement door and listens to his favourite group.

Andy! Andy! Come up here right now!

9

Half an hour later, Andy hears his sister scream. He thinks Emily is angry because he is listening to her CDs.

10

But when Andy opens the door, he sees a cloud of smoke coming from the kitchen. He runs upstairs and sees his mom taking the blackened pizzas out of the oven. Then she turns off the oven.

What did you do? Why did you set the oven at 500°?

I'm really sorry, Mom. I just wanted to make two pizzas for my friends. I doubled everything, the toppings, the temperature and the time.

11

Andy feels terrible about what he did.

12

Honey, you made a terrible mistake. We're lucky I came home in time. You can double the ingredients but you never double the temperature. It stays the same.

13

Andy and his mom clean the oven together.

14

Andy decides to make sandwiches for his friends. His mother and sister help him.

Next time I make pizza, you can watch.

AFTER THE STORY

1 **What happened?**
- Retell the story with your teammates.

I think I have the first sentence.

Can you read it, please?

"It's Friday and Andy is planning a party."

Yes, that's it.

2 **Think about it.**

Andy is a good cook.

Mrs. Kennedy is very patient.

- Do you agree or disagree? Why? Find reasons in the story.

3 **Compare.**
- Have you ever had a problem in the kitchen?
- Are you like Andy or very different?

UNIT 2 Heroes

A There are different kinds of heroes:
- ★ celebrities
- ★ ordinary people
- ★ animals
- ★ fictional characters

Find examples for each category.

B Find the pictures that show
- actors
- a superhero
- brave people
- an athlete
- a dangerous job
- family or friends
- musicians
- a book character
- a volunteer
- an animal

C Who is your hero?
Who is your partner's hero?

LOOKahead

❶ What makes a hero?

A hero has special abilities and talents...

KEY LANGUAGE

He **can** skate really fast.
He**'s good at** scoring goals.
He **practices** really hard.

...and certain personal qualities.

KEY WORDS

He's... ...disciplined ...fast ...and talented.

 A Why are they heroes? Find the reasons.
Your teacher will give you the information you need.

B What makes **your** hero special?

❷ You're a hero!

Sometimes heroes receive medals.

Athletes receive medals because they can perform a sport extremely well.

Other people receive medals because they are very brave.

Volunteers receive medals because they help others.

Jenny, Michael, Melissa and Enrico have some ideas about medals, too.

I deserve a medal because I babysit my little brother and I can think of lots of good games.

I deserve a medal because I'm good at delivering the paper on time.

I deserve a medal because I practice the piano for an hour every day.

I deserve a medal because I'm brave and I help my dad in the kitchen.

- Why do they deserve medals?
- Do you deserve a medal? Why?
- Create medals for yourself and the people you know.

3 Hero info

A Look at the four articles on these pages.
Find each hero's name and age, and a special detail for each one.
Your teacher will give you a sheet to complete.

1

The Chicoutimi Comet

This is Marc Gagnon. He was born in
Chicoutimi on May 24, 1975. He speaks
English and French. His hobbies are
computers, cars and anything with speed.
That makes sense because…

2

VidKid

Her real name is Sarah Jones
and she is 13 years old.
On weekdays, she goes to school,
does her homework – all the
usual activities. But she has
a secret identity. On weekends…

 **KEY WORDS**

speed	**That makes sense.**	**free** (verb)	**newspaper**	**foster family**
	It's logical.	liberate		parents who look after children from other families

3

Free the Children

This is Craig Kielburger. He was born in Toronto on December 17, 1982. Craig's special activity started when he was just 12 years old. He was looking in the newspaper for his favourite comics...

4

A Friend for Life

This is a picture of Gizmo, a very special capuchin monkey. When she was a baby, she lived with a foster family. Then she went to school and learned to do many things. Now Gizmo is 19 years old and she has a lot of responsibilities...

B Choose one of the heroes.
Your teacher will give you the rest of your hero's story.
Share the new information with your teammates.

C Which hero is your favourite? Why?

4 FUN FACTS

A Read the questions. Think about possible answers.

1 Who ran across Canada with an artificial leg?

2 How many points did Wayne Gretzky score in his NHL career?

3 Name a Canadian comic-book superhero.

4 If you see **hero** on a menu, what is it?

5 How long does a police dog go to school?

B Your teacher will give you an answer sheet.

- Discuss the choices with your teammates.
- Choose an answer for each question.
- Mark your score.

FUN FACTS RATING	
4 - 5	You're super!
2 - 3	A heroic score
0 - 1	Oops!

look up to

Enrico **looks up to** his grandfather. He helps Enrico with his Math homework and he's always patient.

cool as a cucumber

Melissa is always very calm when she skates. She's **cool as a cucumber**.

GO for it!

My hero

GRAMMAR POWER

To review the simple present, third person singular, see page 142.

A Read the two texts. Answer the questions.

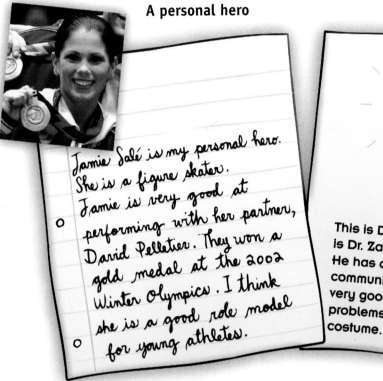

A personal hero

Jamie Salé is my personal hero. She is a figure skater. Jamie is very good at performing with her partner, David Pelletier. They won a gold medal at the 2002 Winter Olympics. I think she is a good role model for young athletes.

A new superhero

This is Dr. Zoo. His regular identity is Dr. Zack Owen and he is a vet. He has a special power. He can communicate with animals. He is very good at understanding their problems. Dr. Zoo wears a funny costume.

1. Who is this personal hero?
2. What kind of hero is she?
3. What is her special ability?

4. Name the superhero's two identities.
5. What are his special abilities?
6. Find another detail about him.

B Write about a personal hero or invent a new superhero. Your teacher will give you instructions and a checklist.

GET HELP

- Look at the models on this page.
- Identify other references.

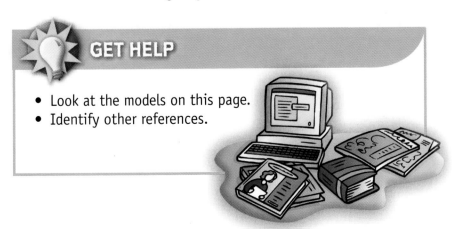

LOOK back

UNIT 3 High School

A Identify the places and things in the pictures. Look at the key words for help.

Last week, Michael and I visited Cartier High School.

This is what we saw.

KEY WORDS

auditorium
computer lab
drinking fountain
elevator
lockers
science lab
social centre
staff room
student radio office

B   What do you see that is the same as in your school?
What do you see that is different?

lookahead

❶ People in school

A Many different people work in a high school.
Find the correct picture for each job description.

I

janitor

A

librarian

B

principal

C

psychologist

1	I look after sick students.
2	I answer the phone and use a computer.
3	I keep the school clean.
4	We study and learn new things.
5	Kids talk to me when they have problems.
6	I'm responsible for everyone in the school.
7	I teach Math and Science.
8	I help you find the book you want.
9	I help students choose their courses.

H

secretary

G

guidance counsellor

D

nurse

E

students

F

teacher

B Who works in your school?
Explain what jobs different people do.

🔑 **KEY LANGUAGE**

Identifying people's jobs
Mr. Ramirez <u>is</u> the librarian.
The principal <u>is</u> Mrs. Barton.
Ms. Davies <u>is</u> a Math teacher.

For teachers, you can also say:
Ms. Huang teach<u>es</u> kindergarten.
Mr. Tremblay teach<u>es</u> French.

② School subjects

A What subjects do kids study in elementary school?
Look at the pictures and key words for ideas.

KEY WORDS

Art
Chemistry
English
French
Geography
Music
Physical Education
Science
Spanish

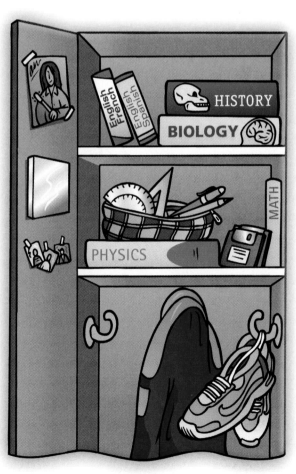

B Here is the inside of a high-school student's locker.
Look for clues that indicate what subjects she studies.

- What subjects are the same as yours?
- What new subjects are you interested in?

3 A strange school

Here is Michael's composition about an imaginary school.

A Complete his text with your classmates' ideas.

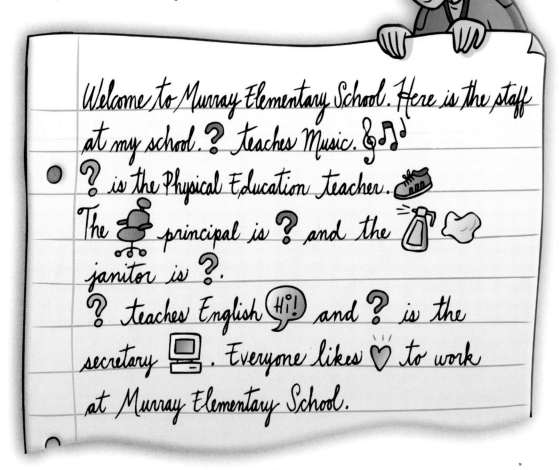

Welcome to Murray Elementary School. Here is the staff at my school. ? teaches Music. ? is the Physical Education teacher. The principal is ? and the janitor is ?. ? teaches English and ? is the secretary. Everyone likes to work at Murray Elementary School.

B Look at the text.
   1. What is the name of Michael's school?
   2. How many jobs are named?
   3. Identify the verb in each sentence.

C Write your composition. Your teacher will give you instructions and a checklist.

GET HELP

Where can you find the key words and key language to help you write your text?

Other ideas

Make a list with your teacher.

4 Timetables

Timetables provide important information for high-school students.

A What information is included in the timetable below?

		Day 1	Day 2	Day 3	Day 4	Day 5	Day 6
1	8:30 to 9:30	Math Room A211	Spanish Room A111	Library Room A112	Math Room A211	Moral Education Room A109	History Room B119
2	9:30 to 10:30	Library Room A112	Math Room A211	Geography Room B216	English Room B129	Geography Room B216	Math Room A211
3	10:30 to 11:30	Geography Room B216	English Room B129	Science Lab B	French Room A214	English Room B129	Phys. Ed. Gym A
	11:30 to 1:00	L U N C H					
4	1:00 to 2:00	French Room A214	Science Lab B	Music Room A209	Phys. Ed. Gym C	History Room B119	French Room A214
5	2:00 to 3:00	History Room B119	French Room A214	English Room B129	Science Lab B	Spanish Room A111	Moral Education Room A109

🔑 KEY LANGUAGE

On Day 1, Math is first period.

Yes, and Library is after Math.

Geography is before lunch.

Right. French is at one o'clock, and History is last period.

 B Practice with your teammates. Your teacher will explain.

 C Prepare a timetable and share it with your partner.

⑤ Getting around

This is the floor plan of a section of Cartier High School.

A On what floor can you find these places?
- the library
- the washrooms
- the principal's office
- the stairs
- the music room
- the art room
- the computer lab
- the staff room
- the cafeteria

Find other rooms mentioned in the timetable.

CARTIER HIGH SCHOOL
Floor plan · Section A

BASEMENT

Stairs

Cafeteria

Girls' washroom
Boys' washroom

Lockers

Elevator

Student radio office

Social centre

Stairs

GROUND FLOOR

Stairs

Girls' washroom
Boys' washroom

Art room A 109

Library A 112

Computer lab A 111

Nurse's office

Elevator

Principal's office

Administration

Staff room

Stairs

MAIN ENTRANCE

FIRST FLOOR

Stairs

Girls' washroom
Boys' washroom

Music room A 209

A 210

A 211

A 212

Elevator

A 213

A 214

A 215

A 216

Stairs

B Use the key language to practice giving directions.

KEY LANGUAGE

On the left.   On the right.   Go straight.   Go upstairs.   Go downstairs.

It's the second door on the left.   It's the last door on the right.

GRAMMAR POWER The future

I **will** go to Nelson High School next year. **I'll** take the bus.
I **will not** walk to school. I **won't** have time.
Will you take the bus too?

⑥ Next year

 BEFORE READING

1 Name the sports in the pictures.
2 Find three school subjects in the text.
3 Who is Melissa's friend?

 **KEY WORDS**

also: too
challenge: a situation when extra effort is necessary
maybe: possibly

Here are Melissa's plans for next year.

Next year, I'll go to Nelson High School, where there is a special sports program. I'll study the usual subjects, like French, Math and Science. I'll also practice my speed skating and train for competitions. My friend Kim will be in the same program – her sport is swimming. In the morning, we'll have our academic courses and, in the afternoon, we'll do our sports training.

Kim and I will take the bus to and from school and we'll eat lunch in the cafeteria. I'm not sure if I'll have time for extra activities, but I really like making videos. Maybe I'll join the Film Club. I know high school will be a challenge, but I'm ready!

AFTER READING

1 What sport does Melissa do?
2 Describe her timetable next year.
3 Does your high school have a special program?
4 What are your plans for next year?

7 Extras

High-school students can join teams and clubs.
Here are some activities offered at Cartier High School.

- Read about the sports activities. When are the practices?
- Read about the special-interest groups. Where do they meet?
- What club or team would you like to join?

Will you join the basketball team?

Will you play in the band?

❽ Dress codes

This is the dress code at Cartier High School.

A Read the rules with your teacher.
Are they the same as for the dress code in your school?

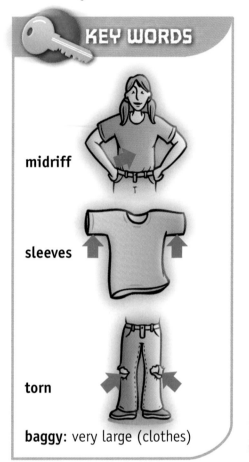

KEY WORDS

midriff

sleeves

torn

baggy: very large (clothes)

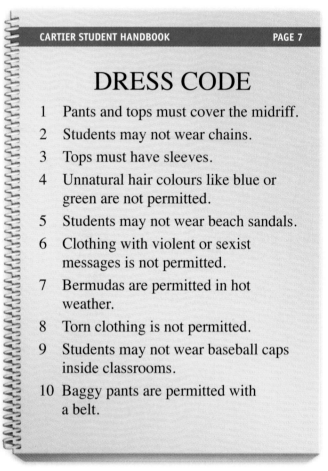

CARTIER STUDENT HANDBOOK   PAGE 7

DRESS CODE

1 Pants and tops must cover the midriff.
2 Students may not wear chains.
3 Tops must have sleeves.
4 Unnatural hair colours like blue or green are not permitted.
5 Students may not wear beach sandals.
6 Clothing with violent or sexist messages is not permitted.
7 Bermudas are permitted in hot weather.
8 Torn clothing is not permitted.
9 Students may not wear baseball caps inside classrooms.
10 Baggy pants are permitted with a belt.

B Discuss these students' clothing with your teammates.
According to the dress code, which clothes are acceptable? Which are not?

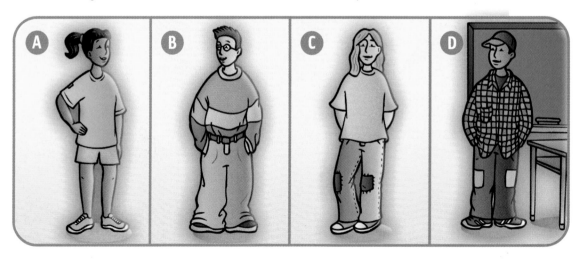

A   B   C   D

C What do you think happens if a student's clothing is not acceptable?
Do you think a school uniform is a good idea?

A high-school puzzle

You have learned a lot about high school.
Use this information to complete a crossword puzzle.
Your teacher will give you clues like these.
Look back through this unit for help.

It has a door.

There are hundreds of these in a high school.

You can put your books and coat in this.

It's usually made of metal.

Design a dream school with your partner.
Imagine a school where the students plan the
building and the timetable, and choose the staff.

1 The building

Design the school building.
You can choose places we usually see in a school
...and think of other possibilities.

Here are some of Michael and Melissa's ideas.

Our dream school has
a computer lab.

There are
two gyms.

There's a
video arcade.

It has
a library.

There is a
skating rink.

There are
fast-food restaurants.

Cool School
(FIRST FLOOR)

LIBRARY

COMPUTER LAB

GYM A

SKATING RINK

GYM B

VIDEO ARCADE

FAST-FOOD RESTAURANTS

2 The timetable

Choose the subjects and activities offered at your dream school.
Set up a timetable.

Here is part of Michael and Melissa's dream timetable.

	DAY 1	DAY 2	DAY 3
8:30 - 9:30	Computer Science	Speed Skating	Italian
9:30 - 10:30	Guitar lessons	Art	Library
10:30 - 10:45	Recess	Recess	Recess
10:45 - 11:45	Science	Video Technique	Swimming
11:45 - 1:15	LUNCH	LUNCH	LUNCH

3 The staff

Decide who will work at your dream school.
You can choose people you know, celebrities or fictional characters.

Here is the staff at Michael and Melissa's dream school.

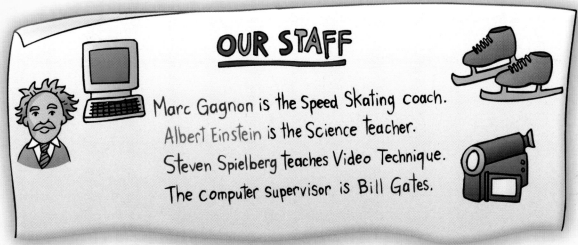

OUR STAFF

Marc Gagnon is the Speed Skating coach.
Albert Einstein is the Science teacher.
Steven Spielberg teaches Video Technique.
The computer supervisor is Bill Gates.

 Describe your dream school to classmates.

The Phone Zone

A Look at the pictures.
Why are these people using the phone?
Imagine their conversations.

B Listen to the recording.
Match each conversation with the correct picture.

C When do you use the phone?
Your teacher has other questions for you.

look ahead

① Fun phone numbers

Is your phone number easy to remember?
Sometimes stores and services choose special phone numbers.
The numbers correspond to letters on the push buttons.
They spell out a message or a word.

A Where do you think these numbers are from?

468-3647 (HOT DOGS)

687-4225 (MUSICAL)

752-8377 (SKATERS)

264-6257 (ANIMALS)

B Your teacher will give you a list.
- Create phone numbers that are easy to remember.
- Share your answers with the class.
- What are your favourites?

② Friends on the phone

A Calling up

KEY LANGUAGE

Enrico phones Michael. Michael's mom, Mrs. Murray, answers the phone.
Listen to the conversation when Michael is at home.

Hello. This is Enrico. Is Michael there, please?

Thanks, Mrs. Murray.

Hello.

Hi, Enrico. Yes, he is. Just a minute, please.

Next, listen to the conversation when Michael isn't at home.

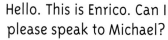

Hello. This is Enrico. Can I please speak to Michael?

Yes. Please ask him to call me.

Thanks, Mrs. Murray. Bye.

Hello.

Hi, Enrico. I'm sorry. He's not here. Can I take a message?

OK. I'll tell him you called. Bye, Enrico.

Oops, wrong number!

Hello. Can I please speak to Michael?

Sorry. Bye.

You have the wrong number.

 Play Call Back. Your teacher will explain.

B Making plans

KEY LANGUAGE

Michael returns Enrico's call.

Hi, Enrico. This is Michael. You called?

Yeah. Do you want to go skating?

Sure, that's a good idea. When?

Is after supper OK?

No. I have a babysitting job at 7:30.

How about tomorrow?

Great. What time?

Is two o'clock OK? I can come to your house at 1:45.

No problem. See you tomorrow.

Bye.

Plan your weekend.
Your teacher will give you a schedule.
• Indicate the times you are "busy."
• Talk to your classmates to complete the rest of the schedule.

Do you want to go swimming?

Sure. Is Saturday OK?

Yes. What time?

How about three o'clock?

Super. See you on Saturday.

3 Just chatting

GRAMMAR POWER The simple past tense

Affirmative form

◆ Add **ed** to form the simple past of regular verbs.
   We watch**ed** Enrico's hockey game yesterday.
   Melissa visit**ed** her grandparents on the weekend.

◆ When the verb ends in **e**, just add **d**.
   We eras**ed** the board before recess.
   I receiv**ed** a CD for my birthday.

◆ When the verb ends in **y**:

   If **y** is preceded by a consonant, change the **y** to **i** and add **ed**.
   Jenny stud**ied** her Math last evening.
   The baby cr**ied** all afternoon.

   If **y** is preceded by a vowel, just add **ed**.
   We play**ed** video games after supper.

◆ Some verbs do not take **ed**. Look on page 145 for a list of irregular verbs.

A Play the Rumours game.
Sometimes a rumour is true, but usually it's not.
Your teacher will help you play Rumours with your teammates.

The first player
reads the rumour.

The second player
gives his version.

The game continues as other players
give their versions too.

She studied
French.

No, she studied
English.

No, he studied
English.

No, he studied
Italian!

GRAMMAR POWER **The simple past tense**

Interrogative form

Use **did** in front of the **subject** and the **base form** of the verb.

Did you call me last night?

Questions	Short answers	
Did you <u>prepare</u> supper yesterday?	Yes, I **did.**	No, I **didn't.**
Did your mom <u>fix</u> your bike?	Yes, she **did.**	No, she **didn't.**

Negative form

Use **did not** or **didn't** before the **base form** of the verb.

I **did not** <u>prepare</u> supper yesterday.	I **didn't** <u>prepare</u> supper yesterday.
My mom **did not** <u>fix</u> my bike.	My mom **didn't** <u>fix</u> my bike.

B Practice with your classmates.

Did you study your Math last night?

No, I didn't.

C Find out what your classmates did on the weekend.
Ask the questions on the Weekend Review sheet.

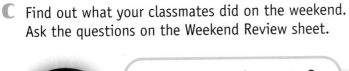

Did you go to the movies?

No, I didn't. Did you play video games?

Yes, I did.

4 FUN FACTS

A Read the questions. Think about possible answers.

1 When did Alexander Graham Bell invent the telephone?
2 How many names were listed in the first phone book?
3 What American city has more phones than people?
4 In what country do most teenagers have cell phones?
5 On what day of the year do people make the most phone calls?

B Your teacher will give you an answer sheet.
- Discuss the choices with your teammates.
- Choose an answer for each question.
- Mark your score.

FUN FACTS RATING	
4 - 5	Mr. Bell is proud of you.
2 - 3	You are a phone fan.
0 - 1	Call the operator!

hang up

Please **hang up**, Melissa. I have to call your dad.

give me a ring

Do you want to go skating?

I don't know. **Give me a ring** after supper.

⑤ Phone help

Sometimes you use the phone to ask for information.
You can call stores, sports centres or cinemas.
You can order from a restaurant too.

KEY LANGUAGE

General information

Do you have the new
Motor Mania video?

Are you open on Sunday?

Time

What time is the movie?

When do you close today?

Price

How much is it,
please?

How much are the skates?

Ordering food

I'd like to order
a pizza, please.

 Get the information you need from your classmates.

Hello. This is
Video-Max.
Can I help you?

Yes. What time
do you close
on weekends?

IMPORTANT NUMBERS

EMERGENCIES 9-1-1	KIDS HELP PHONE 1-800-668-6868
• Call 9-1-1 in a real emergency. • Speak slowly and calmly. • Give your name and address. • Explain the problem.	This is a free service just for kids who need help because of depression, abuse or any other problem. You can call 24 hours a day in English or French. It is not necessary to give your name or tell your family. All calls are confidential.

⑥ Look in the book

Today it's easy to find someone's phone number or address.
You have to know the person's first and last names.

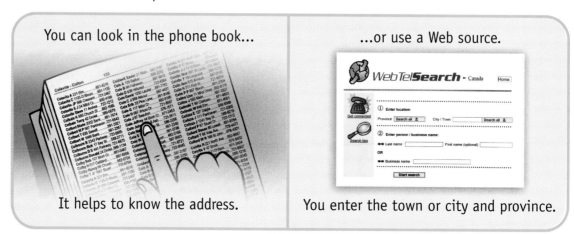

You can look in the phone book...

It helps to know the address.

...or use a Web source.

You enter the town or city and province.

Long ago, people just had one name.
Sometimes this caused a lot of confusion.

Last names or family names were created to help identify people.
At first, family names were related to specific things...

...the person's occupation

Butcher   **Smith**   **Shepherd**

...a place

Hill
a person living near a hill

French
a person from France

Scott
a person from Scotland

...the person's father

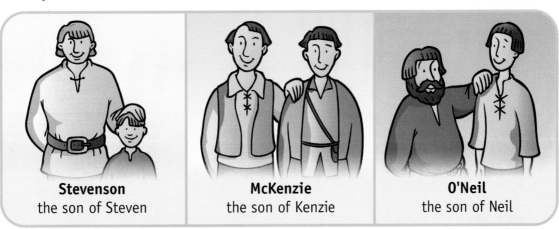

Stevenson
the son of Steven

McKenzie
the son of Kenzie

O'Neil
the son of Neil

...a nickname

Russell
a person with red hair

Long
a person who is tall

Whistler
a person who whistles

These names still exist today.
What are the origins of these names?

- Cook
- Davidson
- Fisher

- McDonald
- Whitehead
- Wood

- Farmer
- English
- Armstrong

- Norman
- Black
- O'Brien

7 Emergency mystery

BEFORE READING

Look at the text.

1 What services can answer a 9-1-1 call?

Look at the pictures.

2 What are the emergency situations in the pictures?

3 Predict who made the call in this story.

KEY WORDS

send: (simple past: sent) make a person or a thing go to a specific place

nobody: no person

bark(ing)

broke: simple past of *break*

The 9-1-1 system is great. It saves lives and stops crimes. It can send the police, the fire department or an ambulance in minutes. But a 9-1-1 call can have a surprising ending too.

One day, a 9-1-1 operator received a strange call. Nobody spoke – the operator just heard a dog barking. He imagined the possibilities: a person in trouble or a dangerous criminal in somebody's home.

The operator traced the call and sent the police immediately. When nobody answered the doorbell, the police broke down the door.

What did they find? Just a dog – no victim, no crime, just a playful pet! The phone was on the floor. Apparently, the dog pressed a button that was programmed to call 9-1-1. This is an emergency story with a happy ending.

AFTER READING

1 Explain how the dog made the call.

2 Imagine the police officers' reaction.

3 Do you think this is a true story? Why?

4 Do you know any 9-1-1 stories? Tell the class.

Phoning up

A Get ready to phone up. Listen to a telephone conversation.

> This is Video-Max. Can I help you?

> Hello. Do you have the new Moon Trek II video?

> Sure. Do you want to reserve a copy?

> Yes, for tonight.

> What's your name and phone number, please?

> Melissa Cole, 671-2453.

> OK. Your copy is reserved until six o'clock tonight.

> Thank you. I'll come before 6:00. Goodbye.

> Goodbye.

B Prepare a dialogue with a partner.
If you have problems:
- Ask your classmates for help.
- Look in your Student Book.

UNIT 5 Shopping

Michael and his friends like to go shopping.
They usually go to Westview Mall.
This is a map of one level at the mall.

A Find these items on the map.

- information booth
- up escalator
- down escalator
- elevator
- public phones
- washrooms
- rest area
- parking garage
- bus stop

GRAMMAR POWER

To review location words, see page 141.

B Match the key words with the stores on the map.
- What can you buy in each store?
- What stores would you like to visit? Why?

C Form shopping teams.
Your teacher will explain.

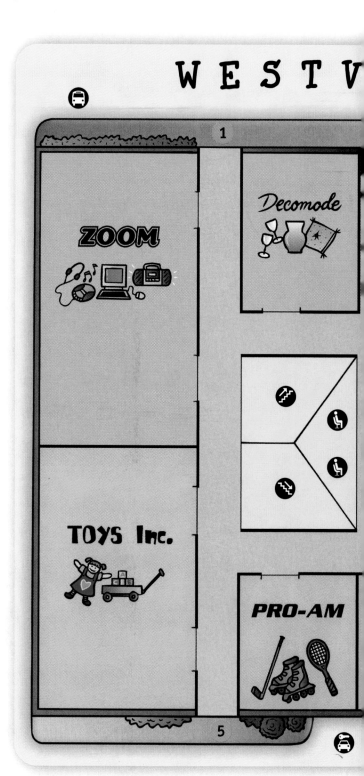

KEY WORDS

candy store	drugstore	grocery store	shoe store
clothing store	electronics store	housewares store	sports store
department store	gift store	jewellery store	toy store

⌐EW MALL

Sparkles

FOOT FAIR

Pharmix

ETC

MAXI-MART

Play Park

Daycare Centre

Freshco

⌐Wishes

Goodies

FOOD COURT

Tacos to go

BEST FRIES

Cookies 'n' Cakes

The Pizza Palace

LOOK ahead

❶ Dollars and cents

We use **coins** and **bills** to pay for things.

A These are the coins and bills we use every day.
 • What is the value of each **coin**?

| a toonie | a loonie | a quarter | a dime | a nickel | a penny |

 • What is the value of each **bill**?

B Name the coins and bills you need to pay for these items.

1 $24.80

2 $9.98

3 $44.55

4 $2.66

5 $18.75

6 $1.49

② FUN FACTS

A Read the questions. Think about possible answers.

1 What bird is on the American quarter?
2 What do we call a person who collects coins?
3 Where was the first bank?
4 What do we call the two sides of a coin?
5 What currency is used in France, Italy and Spain?

B Your teacher will give you an answer sheet.

- Discuss the choices with your teammates.
- Choose an answer for each question.
- Mark your score.

FUN FACTS RATING	
4 - 5	You're a sharp shopper.
2 - 3	You have good cents!
0 - 1	Check your change.

broke

I'm **broke**.

bucks

How much was your new book?

Ten **bucks**, plus tax.

3 Your money

A Money comes in.
- Match the pictures with the key words.
- What are other ways to get money?
- How do you get your money?

B Money goes out.
This is how Enrico spends his money.
Your teacher will tell you what Enrico buys.
- Find the category for each item.

Sports and activities

Things to eat

Entertainment

Things to buy

- Give other examples for each category.
- How do you spend your money?

❹ Budgets

A Keeping track

This is a page from Enrico's budget book. It helps him keep track of his money every month.

NOVEMBER

DATE	IN	OUT	REASON	BALANCE
Nov. 1	–	–	balance from October	$25.00
Nov. 6	$7.50		babysitting	$32.50
Nov. 8	$10.00		allowance	$42.50
Nov. 12		$12.68	present for Dad	$29.82
Nov. 15	$10.00		allowance	$39.82

- What information does he put in his budget book?
- How much money did he receive during this time?
- How much money did he spend?

Help Enrico keep track of his money for December. Your teacher will give you the facts.

B Saving up

Suppose you want to buy something that costs a lot of money. You can calculate **how long** you have to save...

Price of the item with taxes

÷

$$$ you can save every month

=

Number of months

...or **how much** you have to save every month.

Price of the item with taxes

÷

Number of months

=

$$$ to save every month

5 The Shopping Game

HOW TO PLAY

Object of the game:
Visit the stores to buy all the items on your list.

1 Write up your shopping list.

- You must have two items from each section of the mall: blue, orange, green and purple.

- You may not have two items from the same store.

2 Place your marker at one of the six entrances and decide who goes first.

3 Pick a card and move your marker around the board. *NOTE: When you enter a store, you stop counting squares.*

4 When you are ready to buy an item, the player on your left is your salesperson. Use the key language on page 70.

5 The first player to finish his or her list wins the game.

Good luck and have fun!

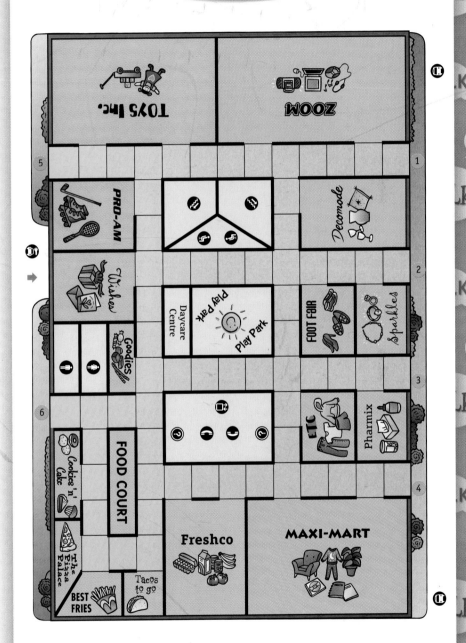

6 Smart shoppers

Melissa wants to buy a new backpack.
She is reading two flyers with backpack ads.

BEFORE READING

1 Name the stores in these ads.
2 Find the prices and the colours for each backpack.
3 Which ad do you like best? Why?

HERO backpacks

QUALITY PRODUCTS
Five-year guarantee*

★ Compartments for cellphone and CD player
★ Reinforced straps and belt
★ Deluxe comfort
★ Comes in purple, grey or black

ONLY **$68.98**

Exclusively at **PRO-AM**

* We repair free of charge.

A **MAXI-MART** special of the week!

Tuffy backpacks

Perfect for active students
Just **$39.95**

You can carry all your school stuff, PLUS
• special pockets for your CD player and CDs
• reflecting tape
• durable metal zippers
• comfortable shoulder straps
• choice of colours: blue, green, black, brown

Offer valid this week only

AFTER READING

1 Compare the backpacks. Your teacher will explain.
2 Which backpack would you buy?
3 What are some other sources of shopping information?

At the mall

A Get ready to go shopping in your classroom.

- With your teammates, make a sign and a poster for your store.
- Show what items are in your store.
  You can...

...draw your own pictures   ...cut out pictures   ...or use a computer.

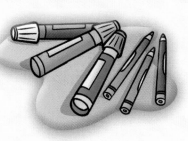

B Now go shopping.

FIRST ROUND

Two members from each team go shopping: they are the **customers**.
They visit other teams and buy what they like in the stores.
The other team members stay at the store:
they are the **salespeople.**
They serve the customers
who come to shop.

SECOND ROUND

When the customers have visited all the stores,
they return to their teams.
The roles are reversed.

LOOKback

TALK TALK TALK TALK TALK TALK TALK TALK TALK TALK TALK TALK TALK TALK TALK TALK TALK TALK TALK

A Story

 GET READY

1 **Take a look.**
- Who is in this story?
- Where does this story take place?

Oooh! Too many pockets!

2 **Use what you know.**
- Ask your partner:
  What's your favourite store?
  Who do you go shopping with?
- Tell your classmates about your partner's answers.

3 **Make a prediction.**
- Look at the pictures.
  What jeans do you think Amy will buy?

 4 **Learn the key words.**

 KEY WORDS

meet

try on

mirror

laugh

free

Amy and Rachel are best friends.

1

Amy loves classical music. She plays the piano and listens to CDs for hours. She loves fast food, especially pizza. Her favourite sport is biking.

2

Rachel is a very good basketball player and she's on the school team. Her favourite food is pizza too. But her favourite music definitely isn't classical.

One activity both girls like is shopping. Here is what they did last Saturday.

3

Riiiing!

Hello?

Hi, Rachel. This is Amy. Do you want to go to the mall today? My grandma gave me $50 and I want to buy a new pair of jeans.

4

Great idea. I want to look at some CDs too. What time?

Is 1:30 OK?

Sure. Let's meet at the Play Park.

OK. See you.

Bye.

5

Amy and Rachel arrived at the Play Park at the same time.

Hi. Are you ready?

Sure. Let's go to ETC.

6

They found the store and started looking at the jeans. A salesperson came over to talk to them.

Can I help you?

Yes. I'm looking for a pair of jeans.

7

What size do you wear?

Um, 26, I think.

What colour do you want?

I'm not really sure.

8

Well, I'll get you a few pairs and you can decide. The changing rooms are in the back.

9

The girls went to the back of the store. The salesperson gave Amy the first pair of jeans to try on.

10

11

The salesperson gave Amy another pair of jeans to try on. She came out of the changing room for the second time.

12

She tried on another pair of jeans and laughed when she looked in the mirror. Rachel laughed too.

13

The salesperson gave Amy another pair of jeans, but still no luck. The girls couldn't stop laughing.

> Oooh! Too many pockets!

14

But suddenly Amy saw a pair of jeans on the floor of the changing room. She liked the colour and style, so she tried them on.

> Hey! Wow! These are the best! They fit and I love the colour. How much are they?

15

> They're free! They're YOUR jeans.

> All right! I guess I don't really need a new pair of jeans. I just saved $50.

16

Rachel and Amy walked out of the store in the direction of the food court.

> Let's get some fries and then we can look at the CDs.

Amy was very happy with her new jeans.

AFTER THE STORY

1 What happened?
- Explain what Amy did in each place.

A

B

C

D

- What was the problem with each pair of jeans?

E   **F**   **G**   **H**

2 Think about it.
- Did Amy really want a new pair of jeans?
- What will she do with her money?

3 Compare.
- Do you like shopping for clothes?
- Are you like Amy or very different?

UNIT 6 The Clothes Line

A What did kids wear in the past?
Match the pictures with the decades in the timeline.

1920s 1930s 1940s

1

2

3

B Compare the clothes they wore with what kids wear today.
What are your favourite clothes?
What do you think kids will wear in the future?

1950s

1960s

1970s

4

5

6

LOOKahead

① Designs

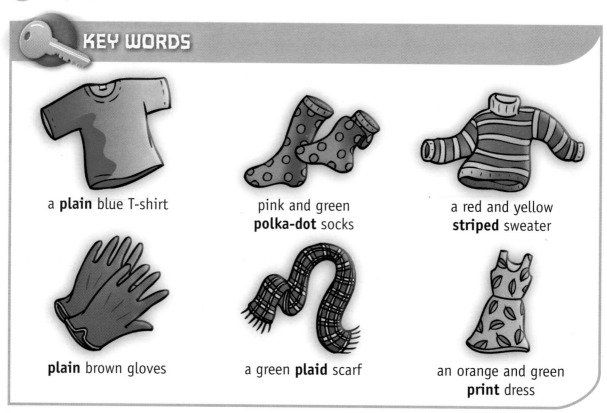

KEY WORDS

a **plain** blue T-shirt

pink and green **polka-dot** socks

a red and yellow **striped** sweater

plain brown gloves

a green **plaid** scarf

an orange and green **print** dress

A Note the position of the **colour** and **design** in each example.
- In what expressions is the design placed first?
- In what expressions is the colour placed first?

B Describe these items.

② Details

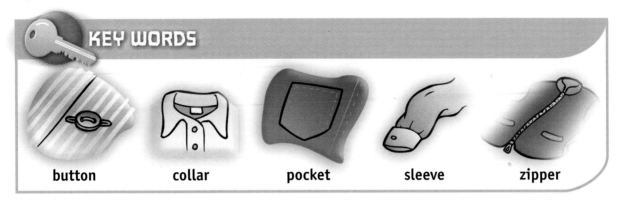

KEY WORDS

button   collar   pocket   sleeve   zipper

A Find Michael's, Jenny's, Melissa's and Enrico's favourite clothing.

I like to wear my red and white print shirt with short sleeves and big pockets.

My favourite item is my green and white striped T-shirt with the little zipper.

I love my blue and yellow print pyjamas with yellow buttons and long sleeves.

I prefer my plain beige pants with lots of pockets and zippers.

1   2   3   4

5   6   7   8

B Look again.
Describe the other items.

③ FUN FACTS

A Read the questions. Think about possible answers.

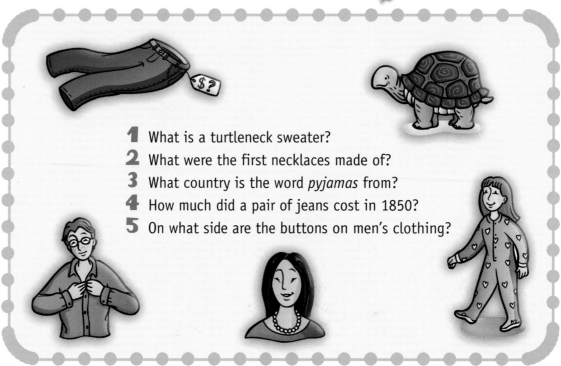

1 What is a turtleneck sweater?
2 What were the first necklaces made of?
3 What country is the word *pyjamas* from?
4 How much did a pair of jeans cost in 1850?
5 On what side are the buttons on men's clothing?

B Your teacher will give you an answer sheet.
• Discuss the choices with your teammates.
• Choose an answer for each question.
• Mark your score.

FUN FACTS RATING	
4 - 5	You have style!
2 - 3	You know clothes.
0 - 1	Do your socks match?

get dressed up

My parents **get dressed up** when they go out for supper.

birthday suit

Stop, Max! You can't go downstairs in your **birthday suit**!

4 Accessories

These items complete an outfit.
Some are useful and others are decorative.

A Match the descriptions with the pictures.

A

a belt

B

a purse

C

earrings

D

a ring

E

glasses

1. You put this jewellery on your ears.
2. This accessory goes under a shirt collar.
3. You put money, keys and other essentials in this.
4. You wear these on sunny days.
5. You wear these to see better.
6. This accessory goes around your waist.
7. It's for telling time.
8. This jewellery goes on your finger.
9. You wear this jewellery on your wrist.
10. You need this when it rains.

F

an umbrella

G

sunglasses

H
a watch

I

a tie

J

a bracelet

 B Learn the words.

 C Play Matching Accessories to practice the new words.
Your teacher will explain.

5 Who's Who?

Your teacher will give you a game board and picture cards.

HOW TO PLAY
Turn the picture cards face down.
One player picks a picture card.
The other players ask questions to guess who it is.

A Get ready to play the game.
Listen to Melissa, Michael, Jenny and Enrico play a game.
Melissa has the card with Nina's picture

2

Is she wearing glasses?

Is she wearing a sweater?

No, she isn't.

Yes, she is. You have another turn.

3

Is she wearing a T-shirt?

Is it a polka-dot T-shirt?

Yes, she is. Go again, Enrico.

No, it isn't.

4

Is it a pink and yellow striped T-shirt?

Yes, I think so. Is it Nina?

Yes, it is. Do you know who it is?

Yes, it is.

B Now play the game.
Take turns asking questions.
Pay attention to the answers.

HAVE FUN!

A fashion show

1 Planning

Choose a secretary to take notes.
Decide with your teammates
- what clothes and accessories to bring
- who can bring what

2 Preparation

Here is an example of what you can write for the fashion show.

What can you bring?

I can bring a cap and a sweater.

I can bring socks and sunglasses.

GRAMMAR POWER

To review the present progressive, see page 143.

This is our model, Melissa. She's very elegant today. She's wearing a red and black striped sweater and plain purple pants. Melissa has big blue sunglasses and an orange and yellow print scarf. She's wearing a green cap and funny red slippers. And to complete her original outfit, Melissa is wearing blue and white polka-dot socks.

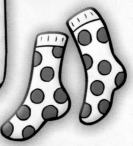

- Look at the items your teammates have brought to class.
- Decide who will be the model.
- Write your text for the fashion show.
  Your teacher will give you instructions and a checklist.

GET HELP

What resources can help you write the text?

3 Presentation

- Dress your model.
- Practice before you present your model to the class.

4 Appreciation

- Take notes as you watch the other teams.
- What did you like in each presentation?

UNIT 7 The Sports Report

A Identify the sports on these pages.
- Are they individual or team sports?
- In what season do you do these sports?
- Are they indoor or outdoor sports?
- Can you think of other sports?

B Practice talking about sports with your classmates.
Use the key language below.

KEY LANGUAGE

Games or team sports	Individual sports
I like to play hockey.	She likes to go skating.
His favourite sport is baseball.	My favourite sport is skiing.

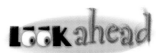

① Clothing and equipment

 Here are some sports items.
Practice the new words.
What sports are they for?

KEY WORDS

ball	ice skates
baseball mitt	in-line skates
bat	jersey
birdie	pads
cap	puck
face guard	racquet
gloves	running shoes
goggles	shorts
helmet	ski boots
hockey stick	spikes

2 Sports Shorts

Get ready to play the game. Learn these expressions.

KEY WORDS

	in a gym	in a pool	at a rink
INDOORS			
OUTDOORS	on a field	on a mountain	on a trail

 Play Sports Shorts.
A teammate will choose a sport. You must guess what it is.

KEY LANGUAGE

Do you play this sport indoors?

Do you need a bat?

Is it a team sport?

Is it football?

No.

No.

Yes.

Yes, that's it. Your turn, Melissa.

3 Favourite sports

Think about it:
- How are skateboarding and snowboarding similar?
- How are they different?

SKATEBOARDING

This sport is a combination of roller-skating and surfing. It began about 40 years ago when kids nailed roller-skate wheels on a plank. Today a skateboarder needs a board with a good truck and polyurethane wheels. It is best to wear a helmet, knee pads, elbow pads and gloves, especially if you do tricks.

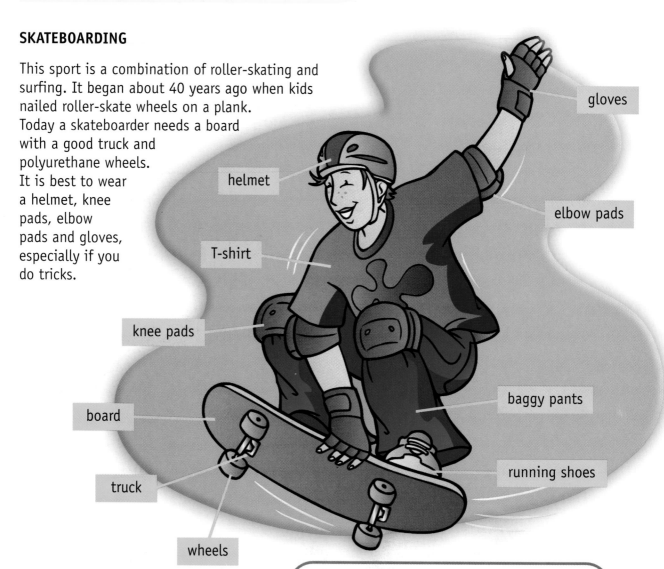

gloves

helmet

elbow pads

T-shirt

knee pads

baggy pants

board

running shoes

truck

wheels

I like to go skateboarding with my friends. We meet in an empty parking lot and practice our ollies and kick-flips. Skateboarding is a blast. I like being with my friends and practicing new tricks.

KEY WORDS

nail (verb)

plank

half-pipe

SNOWBOARDING

Snowboarding is a mix of surfing, skiing and skateboarding. A snowboard is similar in shape to a surfboard but has bindings to hold the feet in place. A snowboarder needs warm clothes, ski goggles and special boots. People of all ages enjoy this sport.

tuque

ski goggles

jacket

gloves

boots

baggy snow pants

board

bindings

Snowboarding is my favourite winter sport. It's an exciting change from skiing. I started snowboarding two years ago. I like watching the pros do tricks on the half-pipe.

AFTER READING

Compare the two sports:
- clothing and equipment
- where they are done
- reasons for popularity
- the sports they combine

4 Play safe!

A Following safety rules is especially important in sports. Read the snowboarding safety tips below and find the matching pictures.

Snow Valley Ski Centre

Snowboarding Safety

1 Learn how to control your speed and how to stop.
2 Never snowboard alone.
3 Watch out for other boarders and skiers.
4 Obey all regulations and signs.
5 Take a break if you are tired; go inside if you are cold.
6 Choose trails that match your ability.
7 Make sure your equipment is in good condition.

B These safety rules apply to other sports too. Give some examples.

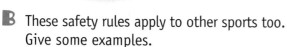

GRAMMAR POWER

To review the imperative, see page 148.

5 FUN FACTS

A Read the questions. Think about possible answers.

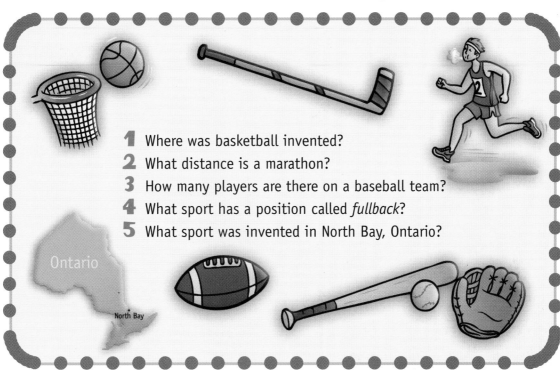

1 Where was basketball invented?
2 What distance is a marathon?
3 How many players are there on a baseball team?
4 What sport has a position called *fullback*?
5 What sport was invented in North Bay, Ontario?

Ontario

North Bay

B Your teacher will give you an answer sheet.
- Discuss the choices with your teammates.
- Choose an answer for each question.
- Mark your score.

FUN FACTS RATING	
4 - 5	You're a sports expert.
2 - 3	You're on track.
0 - 1	Time out!

a true-blue fan

HOME 0   VISITORS 5

He sure is **a true-blue fan.**

jump the gun

Oops! I **jumped the gun**.

6 Sports Rally

Play this game with your teammates.

HOW TO PLAY
- The first player picks a card and reads the first clue.
- The other players get **two** chances to guess the answer.

- If they don't give the correct answer, the first player reads the second clue.
- The other players get **one** chance to guess the answer.

- The game continues with the last two clues if necessary.
- Your teacher will explain how to count your points.

CLUES

1 It's a winter sport.
2 There are six players on a team.
3 The players need skates and pads.
4 You play this sport in an arena.

Answer: Hockey

Favourite sports

Write about a sport you enjoy.
It can be **a sport you like to do**...

or **a sport you like to watch**.

- Look at your notes.
  Look through the pages of this unit.
  What information will you include?

- Write your composition.
  Your teacher will give you
  instructions and a checklist.

- Illustrate your text.

GET HELP

Identify other references
you can use to write
and illustrate your text.

look back

UNIT 8 Friends

What qualities do you look for in a friend?
- Look at the pictures.
- Write down your preferences in order of importance.

1 A person who listens

2 A person who doesn't tell secrets

3 A person who shares

4 A person who likes the same things I do

5 A person I can depend on

6 A person who helps me when I have problems

- What quality is at the top of your list?
- Compare your list with a classmate's list.
- Think of another quality that makes a good friend.

❶ Personalities

A These key words describe different aspects of our personalities.
- Match the key words with the pictures.
- Name a person you know who fits each word.
- Which words describe you?

artistic	impatient
athletic	musical
forgetful	quiet
funny	sociable
generous	studious
helpful	talkative

1 Jenny is...

2 Enrico is...

3 Melissa is...

4 Enrico is...

5 Michael is...

6 Melissa is...

7 Jenny is...

8 Michael is...

9 Jenny is...

10 Melissa is...

11 Michael is...

12 Enrico is...

...and then I said that I knew what she was talking about. Just the other day, I was...

B Talk to your classmates about their personalities.

C Work with a partner. This person will be your partner for other activities too. Ask your partner to describe his or her personality. Write down the answers.

one hundred and one **101**

② Favourites

A Ask your partner about his or her preferences.
Write down your partner's answers.

B Look back to page 5, Making connections.
Do you remember your answers?
Have your preferences changed?

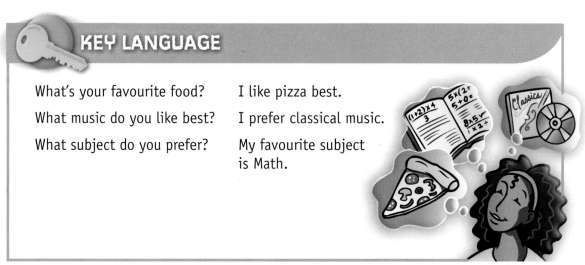

③ People poems

Write a poem using the letters in your partner's name.
Here are some ideas:

Descriptions	Actions	Or a combination
Super Optimist Patient Happy Interesting Energetic	Plays basketball Acts silly Understands Math Loves chocolate	Knows Spanish Adventurous Reads comics Eats chips Never nervous

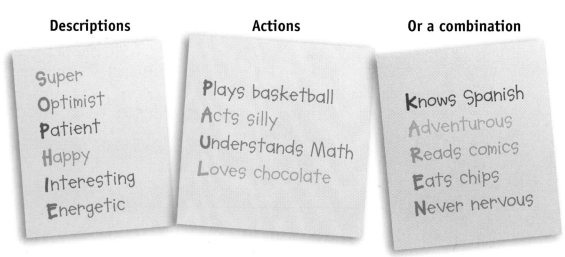

Need help?
- Talk to your partner and to other classmates.
- Talk to your teacher.
- Look in the dictionary.

4 Special interests

Everybody has special interests. Some kids take lessons, some have collections. Others have hobbies they really like.

 Listen to Jenny, Michael, Melissa and Enrico describe their special interests. Find the correct picture for each person.

AFTER LISTENING

 Ask your partner about his or her special interests and record the answers.

Do you have a collection?

What do you collect?

Do you take lessons?

What's your hobby?

5 At home

A Find out about your partner's family and pets.
What questions can you ask?
Here are some ideas.

Name

Name

Name

Name

Record the answers.

B Do you have a special treasure?
Describe it to your partner and to other classmates.

6 Friends and feelings

A Friendship has its ups and downs.
- Find the pictures that show the good times.
- Find the pictures that show the hard times.

A

B

C

1. I'm excited when we watch a hockey game together.

2. I'm lonely when my friend goes to summer camp.

3. I'm angry when we fight.

4. I'm worried when my friend is in the hospital.

5. I'm proud when my friend wins a medal.

6. I'm disappointed when my friend doesn't call.

D

E

F

B Match the pictures with the sentences in the middle of the page. What words describe the feelings?

C Describe situations when you had these feelings.

A class yearbook

Use your notes to write a yearbook text about your partner.

A Here are two examples.

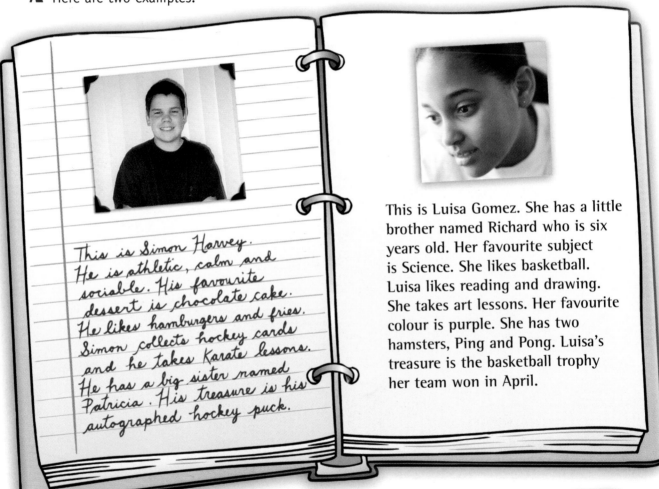

This is Simon Harvey. He is athletic, calm and sociable. His favourite dessert is chocolate cake. He likes hamburgers and fries. Simon collects hockey cards and he takes Karate lessons. He has a big sister named Patricia. His treasure is his autographed hockey puck.

This is Luisa Gomez. She has a little brother named Richard who is six years old. Her favourite subject is Science. She likes basketball. Luisa likes reading and drawing. She takes art lessons. Her favourite colour is purple. She has two hamsters, Ping and Pong. Luisa's treasure is the basketball trophy her team won in April.

Look at the text about Simon.
- What sentence describes Simon's personality?
- What sentence tells us about his family?
- Identify the verb in each sentence.
- When do you use *he*?
- When do you use *his*?

Look at the text about Luisa.

- What sentences tell us about Luisa's favourites?
- What sentences explain her special interests?
- Identify the verb in each sentence.
- When do you use **she**?
- When do you use **her**?

GRAMMAR POWER

To review word order, see page 139.

B Write your text. Your teacher will give you instructions and a checklist.

GET HELP

What resources can you use?
Make a list with your teacher.

IMPORTANT
Bring a photo of yourself for your partner's final copy.

Now you can read all about your classmates in the class yearbook.

look back

A Story

1 **Take a look.**
- Who is the main character?
- What sport does he play?
- Who is the narrator?
- How are these two characters connected?
- Find the names of two other characters.

2 **Think back.**
- What is the best thing you have done for a friend?
- What is the best thing a friend has done for you?

3 **Make a prediction.**
- Look at picture No. 9. What is Jeff anxious about?
- Will Jeff recover?
- Will he play his favourite sport again?

4 **Learn the key words.**

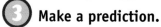

KEY WORDS

| field | dizzy | fall (fell) | carry (carried) |
| dirt | shave | bald | recover |

THE BALD EAGLES

1 Hello. My name is Dr. Elizabeth Tan. I work in a big children's hospital. I'd like to tell you about a patient I had about three years ago. He was a special boy with special friends.

2 Jeff Mason was twelve years old and a regular kind of kid. He loved listening to his favourite music groups and he really liked video games.

3 But soccer was his all-time favourite activity. Jeff practiced for hours and he was a good player. He played for the West City Eagles.

4 His teammates were his friends too. After the games they went for pizza or hamburgers together.

5

But one day, in the middle of an important match, Jeff suddenly stopped running. He felt dizzy and extremely tired. He tried to run, but he fell. His coach and his dad rushed onto the soccer field.

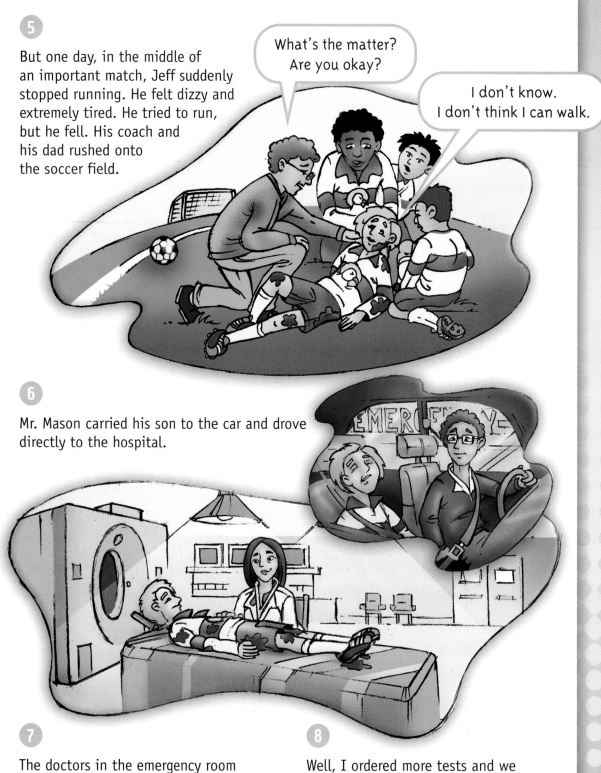

What's the matter? Are you okay?

I don't know. I don't think I can walk.

6

Mr. Mason carried his son to the car and drove directly to the hospital.

7

The doctors in the emergency room examined Jeff and then called me. I am a specialist. I will never forget the first time I saw Jeff – he was covered in dirt from head to foot.

8

Well, I ordered more tests and we discovered that Jeff was very sick with cancer. He had an operation to remove the tumour and chemotherapy treatments to make sure the cancer didn't return.

9

Jeff was anxious about these treatments. He knew they would make his hair fall out.

10

But his teammates decided to help. Before Jeff went for his first treatment, they all went to the barbershop – even Tom Armstrong, the coach – and asked for special haircuts. The barber shaved their heads!

11

When Jeff saw his bald friends, he really laughed. And when Jeff lost his hair after chemotherapy, he looked just like the rest of the team so he didn't feel so bad.

12

His teammates also decided to change the name of the soccer team.

THE BALD EAGLES

13

The story about Jeff and his friends was in magazines, newspapers and on TV. All the reporters asked the same question:

Why did you do this?

It's the new style for soccer players.

We don't like washing our hair.

14

Jeff's friends joked about it, but everyone knew they had shaved their heads to help Jeff.

15

Today Jeff is fine. His parents are sure his friends' support helped him to recover. Jeff is 15 now. He listens to his favourite groups, enjoys games on his computer and plays soccer. He's the top scorer on his team.

And he has a picture of the West City Bald Eagles on the wall in his bedroom.

AFTER THE STORY

1 **What happened?**
- Use the pictures to tell Jeff's story.

A

B

C

D

E

F

G

THE BALD EAGLES

H

I

- What is your favourite part of the story? Why?

2 **Think about it.**
- Imagine how Jeff feels at different times in the story.
  Here are some ideas.

happy	touched	sad	sick	nervous
scared	proud	anxious	confused	relieved

3 **Compare.**
- Would you shave your head for a friend?
- Suggest other things you could do for a friend in Jeff's situation.

PROJECT 2 Operation Keys

Think back.
What did you learn in English class this year?
Review what you know by creating a game, quiz or puzzle.

A Make up questions.

1 Brainstorm with your teammates.
Look for ideas in your Student Book.

We talked about shopping.
Do you remember?

Sure. We learned how to say prices.

And the names of coins.

I know — that was Unit 5.
Let's see...page 66.

2 Take notes.

Name of Canadian coins
Stores
Spending money

3 Make up questions based on your notes.

Hmm, Canadian coins.
Can you think of a question?

Sure. "What do we call a $1 coin?"

Great, Jenny.

B Use the questions you created.

1 You can invent a game.
- Draw and colour a game board.
- Write your questions...

...right on the board

...or on pieces of paper.

WHAT DO WE CALL A $1 COIN?

- Include other instructions for playing the game.
  Here are some examples:

Go back
3 squares.

Go forward
2 squares.

Miss a turn.

Take another
turn.

Change places
with another
player.

- Players use move cards to play.
- Prepare an answer sheet for reference.

2 You can make a crossword puzzle.
- Use the answers to your questions to make a crossword puzzle. Graph paper makes the job easier.
- Use the questions as clues.
- Give the finished puzzle to your classmates. They can ask you for help.

L
O
O
N
NICKEL
E

What do we call a $1 coin?
It starts with an L.

I think that's
LOONIE.

Yeah, that's it.

TALK
TALK
TALK
TALK
TALK
TALK
TALK
TALK
TALK
TALK
TALK
TALK
TALK
TALK

3 You can prepare a quiz sheet.
- Write your questions on a sheet of paper.
- Exchange sheets with another team.
- Look in your Student Book for help.

QUIZ

1. Where is Marc Gagnon from?

Do you remember Marc Gagnon?

Yes, I think he's in the Heroes unit. Let's look.

4 You can organize a game show.
- Collect everybody's questions.
- Decide how to play and count points.

Melissa 4   Sam 4   Enrico 3   Jasmin 5

emcee

contestants

audience

Special Occasions

Halloween

1 A Halloween party

A Michael is having a Halloween party.
Identify as many Halloween costumes and decorations as you can.
Make a list with your teammates.

B Count your points.
How did you do?

❷ Trick-or-treat for UNICEF

BEFORE READING

1 Have you ever collected for UNICEF?

2 What is the money used for?

3 Estimate how much money is collected in your school.

Look at Michael on page 118. He is wearing an orange and black UNICEF box.

Kids all across Canada collect money for UNICEF (the United Nations Children's Fund) when they go trick-or-treating on Halloween. This organization helps children in over 160 countries and territories around the world.

The money that is collected is used to provide health care, nutrition, education, protection and other things that children need.

KEY WORDS

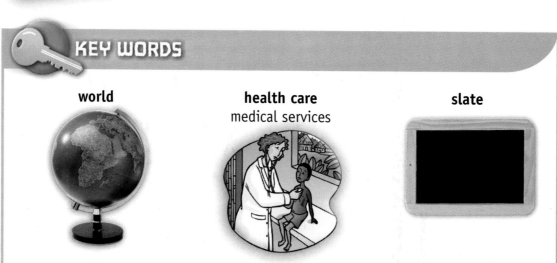

world

health care
medical services

slate

emergency
a serious or dangerous situation

children's rights
what children are supposed to have: food and education, for example

Many countries do not have enough schools. More than 120 million children in the world cannot go to school. UNICEF has created a special kit to help teachers in these countries. It is called the Teacher's Emergency Package (TEP). It is a box with basic reading and mathematics materials for 80 students. The kit also contains a blackboard, slates for the children, chalk, pencils, copybooks and educational games. This "school in a box" costs about $200, depending on where it is used.

When you collect money for UNICEF at Halloween, you are helping to protect children's rights all over the world, including the right to education.

AFTER READING

1 Compare what is in the TEP kit with what is in your school.
2 Do you have any suggestions for what to include in a TEP kit?
Remember: it must be small and must not cost a lot of money.

After Halloween
3 How much money was collected for UNICEF at your school?
Calculate how many TEP kits UNICEF can buy with the money collected.

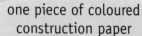

❸ Halloween masks

Make masks to decorate your classroom or home.

This is what you will need:

one piece of coloured construction paper

scissors

glue

a pencil

your classmates

your creativity

This is how to make the mask:

1 Fold the construction paper in half vertically.

2 Trace the shape of half a head on the OUTSIDE edge of the folded paper. Don't forget the ears. Cut out the shape.

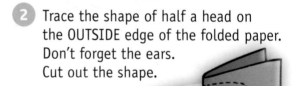

3 Trace the mouth and nose on the FOLD and cut them out.

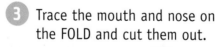

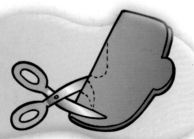

4 Fold the top down. Trace and cut out the eyes.

5 Unfold your creation and decorate it with different coloured construction paper. Ask your classmates for help.

You can put your masks on the bulletin board, on a wall or on a window.

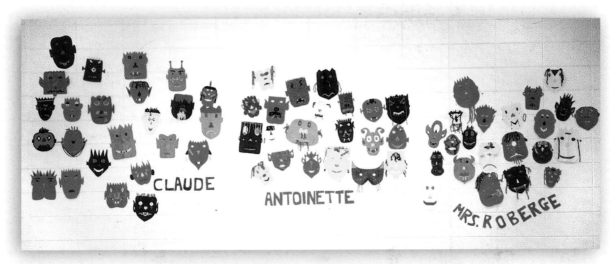

Christmas

❶ Making sense of Christmas

At Christmas time, there are special things you can...

see   hear   smell

taste   touch

- Identify the pictures below.
- Which senses give you information about these Christmas items?

② Presents

This is a flyer from the Maxi-Mart Department Store.
It has lots of ideas for Christmas gifts.

SPECIAL — NO TAX TODAY!

A Holiday boxer shorts

$6.98

B Assorted chocolates

$4.50

C Diary with matching pen

$4.98

D Fruit soaps

99¢

E Felt markers

$4.98

F Coffee mugs

$4.98

G Christmas teddy bear

$6.98

H Colouring book and crayons

$2.99

I Miniature vases

$5.00

J Festive socks

$3.99

K Hair bands and barrettes

$1.98 TO $4.98

L Piggy banks

$6.49

- Jenny has $25 for presents. Help her find the perfect gift for everyone on her list.

- What gifts would you choose for your friends and family?

Mom
David
Dad
Melissa

3 Christmas around the world

 **BEFORE READING**

What do you know about Santa Claus?

Read about Christmas traditions in different countries.

1

2

In Italy it is Befana, a good witch, who brings presents to the children. She carries a broom and gives her gifts on January 5. She wears a scarf on her head and carries a big bag on her back. Sometimes Befana sweeps the floor with her broom before she leaves the house.

Sinterklaas is from Holland. He wears a long red robe and he has a white beard. Sinterklaas rides a white horse when he visits on December 6. Sometimes Dutch children leave carrots and hay for his horse.

KEY WORDS

apron

broom

You **sweep** the floor with a broom.

goat

hay

Babushka is from Russia. She is an old woman with a basket of presents over her arm. She wears a long cape and an apron as she walks from house to house. People make decorations called *baba* dolls to put on the Christmas tree in honour of Babushka.

In Spain, the Three Wise Men bring gifts to the children on January 6. Their names are Melchior, Balthazar and Gaspar. The children's favourite is Balthazar because they think he is the one who brings the gifts. Children put their shoes beside a window in their home. They place hay and carrots in their shoes for the Wise Men's horses.

Tomte the Christmas gnome is from Sweden. During the year, he protects the home and family. But on December 24 he comes out of his house under the floor. Tomte rides a goat and carries a sack over his shoulder. He gives presents to everyone, sometimes with funny poems.

AFTER READING

1 Complete a chart to compare Santa Claus and the other characters.

2 Which character is your favourite? Why?

3 Create a new Christmas character.

4 FUN FACTS

- Read the questions. Think of possible answers.
- Your teacher will give you an answer sheet.
  Discuss the choices with your teammates and choose an answer.

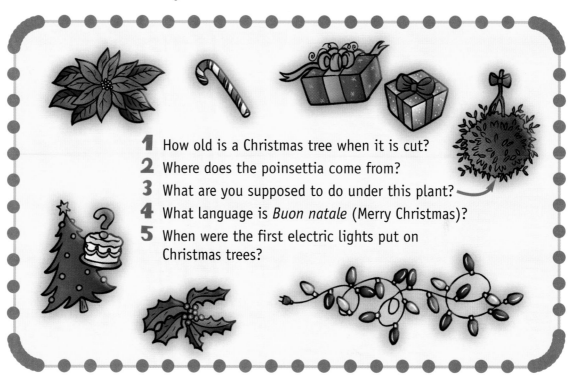

1 How old is a Christmas tree when it is cut?
2 Where does the poinsettia come from?
3 What are you supposed to do under this plant?
4 What language is *Buon natale* (Merry Christmas)?
5 When were the first electric lights put on Christmas trees?

5 Christmas riddles

Can you think of the answers?

A What do monkeys sing at Christmas time?

B Where does Santa Claus stay when he's on vacation?

C What reindeer is not very polite?

D What do Santa's helpers learn in school?

6 Christmas Bingo

Identify the pictures on this page.
Play Christmas Bingo with your classmates.
Have fun!

Merry Christmas!

Valentine's Day

A What do you do on Valentine's Day?

Do you make a card?

Do you make cookies?

Do you buy flowers?

Many people buy chocolates on Valentine's Day. Chocolate companies make millions of boxes of chocolates for this special day.

Companies use a special code so people will know what is inside every box of assorted chocolates. They make the chocolates in different shapes and put different designs on the top.

Then, they place a little card in the box with pictures to show what the shapes and designs mean.

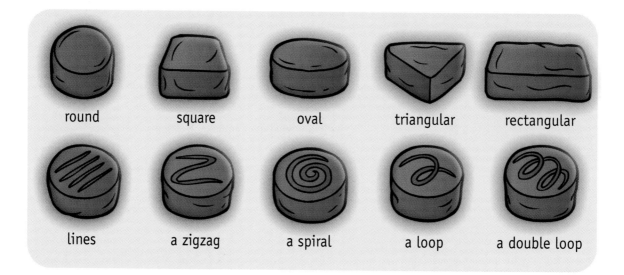

round	square	oval	triangular	rectangular
lines	a zigzag	a spiral	a loop	a double loop

B Here is a box of Valentine's chocolates. Look at the picture card and answer the questions below.

Marshmallow nut

Coconut crunch

Orange cream

Peanut butter

Lemon coconut

Coffee cream

Fudge deluxe

Cherry surprise

1. What chocolate is square with a double loop?
2. What chocolate is round with a spiral?
3. What chocolate is triangular with a loop?
4. Describe the marshmallow nut chocolate.
5. Describe the peanut butter chocolate.

C Create a chocolate.

This is a cherry fudge chocolate. It's triangular with a zigzag.

Happy Valentine's Day!

Reference Section

KEY LANGUAGE

GRAMMAR POWER

STRATEGIES

THE WRITING PROCESS

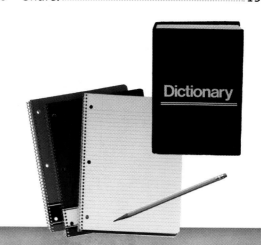

KEY LANGUAGE

1 Asking for help

Help me, please.
Can you help me?
I need help.
How do you say *souris*
in English?
How do you spell *mouse*?
What does *binder* mean?
I have a problem.

2 Asking for clarification

Repeat that, please.
Say that again, please.
I don't understand.
Please speak up.
Pardon?
What do you mean?

3 Asking for more time

Wait.
Hold it.
Wait a minute.
Just a minute, please.
I'm not ready.

I'm not sure.
Let's see now.
Let me think about it.
Well...
What about you?

4 Using other words — WHEN YOU DON'T KNOW ITS NAME...

A NAME ITS CATEGORY.

It's a fruit.

It's an animal.

B DESCRIBE IT.

It's long and yellow.

It has six legs.

C SAY WHERE IT IS.

You see it in the bathroom.

It's in a classroom.

D SAY WHAT YOU DO WITH IT.

You use it to draw a circle.

You eat with it.

5 Offering help

Can I erase
the board?
Can I help?
Can I help you?
Need help?
Do you need help?

6 Asking for permission

Can we work on
the computer?
May I close
the window?
Is it OK if we
take the books?

7 Asking for things

Can I have a piece of paper, please?
Can I borrow your eraser?
Do you have a ruler?
I'd like a sandwich, please.
I want some cookies, please.

8 Being polite and apologizing

Please.   Sorry.
Thank you.   I'm sorry.
Thanks for your help.   Excuse me.
You're welcome.

9 Expressing feelings

How do you feel?
I'm happy.   I'm sad.
I feel great.   I'm angry.
I'm excited.   I'm disappointed.
I'm proud of my project.

10 Talking about capabilities

I can ski well.
I'm good at skateboarding.

I can't draw.
I'm not so good at swimming.

Can you play basketball?
Are you good at painting?

11 Team talk

A DURING AN ACTIVITY OR A GAME

Who goes first?
I go first.
I start.
I'm next.
Whose turn is it?
Not too loud!
Five minutes left.
We have ten minutes.

Are you ready?
Let's listen to Melissa.
I have a suggestion.
Do you have an idea?
Great idea!
I like that.
I like your suggestion.

B AFTER AN ACTIVITY OR A GAME

Good job.
Nice work.
We're a good team.
You're a great partner.

Congratulations!
That was fun.
Way to go!
Let's play again.

12 Agreeing and disagreeing

A SAYING "YES"

Sure.
Right.
All right.
Me too.
Certainly.
Of course.
That's right.
I agree.

B SAYING "NO"

No way.
Not that.
Not me.
I don't think so.
Never.
I don't agree.
I disagree.

C EXPRESSING UNCERTAINTY

Maybe.
I'm not sure.

13 Working together

A SUGGESTIONS

Let's look in the dictionary.
How about writing
the text first?

B INVITATIONS

Do you want to be my partner?
Want to colour the poster?
Who wants to draw the pictures?

C ASKING FOR AN OPINION

What do you think?
What's your opinion?
Do you agree?
What about you?

D EXPRESSING AN OPINION

I think it's great.
I think Enrico is right.
I agree.
I disagree.

14 Preferences

A ASKING ABOUT PREFERENCES

What's your favourite subject?
What sport do you like best?
What colour do you prefer?

What do you want?
What about you?

B EXPRESSING PREFERENCES

My favourite subject is Math.
I like tennis best.
I prefer turquoise.
I love red.
I don't like orange.
I want a pizza, please.
I'd like a piece of pie.

I like blue.
I really like purple.
I hate brown.

GRAMMAR POWER

1 Articles

THE

- When talking about a specific person or thing, use **the**.
- Use **the** for the singular and plural.
  The book about pizza is interesting.
  I like **the** shoes you are wearing today.

A, AN

- When talking about something in general, use **a** (before a consonant) or **an** (before a vowel).
- Use **a** or **an** only before a singular noun.
  I have **a** new computer.
  An orange is a good snack.
  BUT
  Oranges are delicious.

2 Question words   ASKING ABOUT...

A PERSON

Who is that?

David Tan.

A THING OR AN ANIMAL

What is in the box?

A new computer game.

A PLACE

Where do you live?

On Second Avenue.

A TIME

When is recess?

At two o'clock.

POSSESSION

Whose eraser is it?

It's Michael's.

A REASON

Why do you like Science?

Because it's interesting.

AGE

How old is he?

He's twelve.

A NUMBER

How many sheets do you need?

Three or four.

A PRICE

How much are those shoes?

They're $39.99.

3 Plurals

A Add **s** to form the plural of most nouns.

pencil ➡ My pencil**s** are in my backpack.

B Add **es** to words ending in **s**, **sh**, **ch**, **x** or **z**.

dish ➡ They wash the dish**es** every day.

C If a word ends in **f** or **fe**, change the **f** to **v** and add **es**.

scarf ➡ We wear scar**ves** when it's cold.

knife ➡ Please put the kni**ves** on the table.

D If a word ends in **y** preceded by a consonant, change the **y** to **i** and add **es**.

story ➡ I like scary stor**ies**.

E If a word ends in **y** preceded by a vowel, just add **s**.

monkey ➡ This book is about two little monkey**s**.

F Some words do not take **s**. They have a special plural form.

child ➡ **children**

man ➡ **men**

woman ➡ **women**

foot ➡ **feet**

tooth ➡ **teeth**

mouse ➡ **mice**

GRAMMAR POWER

4 Punctuation

- Use a **capital letter** for the first word in a sentence.

We finished our work on time.

- Use a **period** at the end of an affirmative sentence.

- Use a **comma** when you make a list in a sentence.

Do you want toast, cereal, pancakes or eggs for breakfast?

- Use a **question mark** at the end of an interrogative sentence.

5 Word order in a sentence

In an affirmative sentence:
The SUBJECT is first.
The VERB is next.
And the REST OF THE SENTENCE follows.

Jenny babysits her brother.

GRAMMAR POWER

6 Possessives and pronouns

My name is Michael. **I** have a puppy.

Your name is Melissa. **You** have a turtle.

His name is Enrico. **He** has a cat.

Her name is Jenny. **She** has a hamster.

Its name is Scruffy. **It** plays with a ball.

Our cat is named Tiger. **We** love **our** cat.

Their hamster is Harry. **They** clean its cage.

FOR NOUNS AND PROPER NOUNS

Singular nouns and names
- Put **'s** after the word or the name.
  The teacher**'s** chair
  Jenny**'s** backpack

Plural nouns
- Put **'** after the word.
  The boys**'** washroom

7 Order of adjectives

ADJECTIVES			NOUN
(1) Quantity	(2) Characteristic	(3) Colour	
many	tiny	purple	flowers
	short	blond	hair

CLOTHING ADJECTIVES				NOUN
(1) Quantity	(2) Characteristic	(3) Colour	(4) Design	
two	beautiful	pink and green	polka-dot	socks
a	plain	yellow		T-shirt

GRAMMAR POWER

8 Location

on the left	**on the right**	**in**
on	**under**	**behind**
beside	**between**	**in front of**

9 Expressions of time

Talking about...	
a day ➡ **on** Saturday	**before** supper
a date ➡ **on** October 24	
a month ➡ **in** March	
a time ➡ **at** three o'clock	**after** supper

Talking about the past	**Talking about the future**
Yesterday	Tomorrow
Last week	Next week
Two days ago	Next month

Talking about frequency

always*  sometimes*  never*

* Place these expressions of time between the subject and verb.
We **always** play video games at Michael's house.

10 The simple present

The simple present is used to describe routine or habitual actions and facts.

A AFFIRMATIVE

I **play** tennis.
You **play** hockey.
She **plays** the piano.
We **play** rugby.
They **play** golf.

In the third person singular:
- For most verbs, add **s**.
- For verbs ending in **s, sh, ch, x, z** or **o**, add **es**.
- For verbs ending in a **consonant + y**, change **y** to **i** and add **es**.
- For **to have**, the form is **has**.

Jenny like**s** shopping.
Michael watch**es** TV after school.

Enrico stud**ies** music.
Melissa **has** a turtle.

B NEGATIVE   Note the contractions.

I **don't** eat meat.
You **don't** eat dessert.
He **doesn't** eat vegetables.
We **don't** eat candy.
They **don't** eat fish.

- Use **does not (doesn't)** for the third person singular.
- Use **do not (don't)** for all other persons.

Jenny **doesn't** have a little sister.
We **don't** understand.

C INTERROGATIVE

Do I have a role?
Do you want this?
Does it match?
Do we start now?
Do they agree?

Yes/no questions
- Use **does** for the third person singular.
- Use **do** for all other persons.

Does Jenny babysit David?
Do you need more time?

Information questions
- Place the question word before **do** or **does**.

When do you watch TV?

11 The present progressive

The present progressive is used to describe actions happening right now.

A AFFIRMATIVE   Note the contractions.

I **am eating** a sandwich.   I**'m** eating...
You **are reading** a book.   You**'re** reading...
Melissa **is wearing** a green cap. She**'s** wearing...
We **are listening** to Enrico.   We**'re** listening...
They **are drawing** pictures.   They**'re** drawing...

The present progressive has two parts: the verb **to be**
and the **main verb**.
Use the present of the verb **to be** (**am**, **is**, **are** or their contracted form).
Add **ing** to the main verb:

* For most verbs, just add **ing**.   She's **visiting** her grandparents.
* For verbs ending in **e**, take off the **e** first.   They're **writing** letters.
* For some short verbs, double the final consonant.   I'm **cu<u>tt</u>ing** out the pictures.

B NEGATIVE   Note the contractions.

* Place **not** after the verb **to be**.
    I **am not** doing my homework.   I**'m not** doing...
    Michael **is not** walking to school. He **isn't** walking...
    You **are not** watching TV.   You **aren't** watching...

C INTERROGATIVE

Yes/no questions
* Invert the subject and the verb **to be**.
    Are you eating your lunch?
    Is the baby crying?
    Are the kids playing outside?

Information questions
* Place the question word first.
    Who is Jenny talking to?
    What are you doing?
    Why are they going home?

12 The simple past

A AFFIRMATIVE

Last weekend...

I clean**ed** my room.
You wash**ed** the dog.
She visit**ed** her grandmother.
We prepar**ed** supper.
They stud**ied** for the test.

- The same verb form is used for all persons.
- For most verbs, add **ed.**
- For verbs ending in **e**, add **d.**
- For verbs ending in a **consonant + y**, change the **y** to **i** and add **ed.**
- Some verbs are irregular and do not follow these rules. See the list on page 145.

We finish**ed** our work.
Michael clos**ed** the door.

Melissa carr**ied** her books.

B NEGATIVE   Note the contractions.

Two days ago...

I **didn't** wash the dishes.
You **didn't** feed the dog.
It **didn't** play outside.
We **didn't** clean our room.
They **didn't** go shopping.

- Use **did not (didn't)** with the <u>base form</u> of the verb for all persons.

We **didn't** <u>see</u> the movie.
She **didn't** <u>finish</u> her homework.

C INTERROGATIVE

Yesterday...

Did I lend you my book?
Did you watch TV?
Did he make his bed?
Did we receive any mail?
Did they win the game?

Yes/no questions
- Use **did** with the <u>base form</u> of the verb for all persons.

Did you <u>study</u> your Math?
Did they <u>watch</u> the game last night?

Information questions
- Place the question word first.

Where did you go on Saturday?

SIMPLE PAST OF SOME IRREGULAR VERBS

Verb	Past	Verb	Past	Verb	Past
to be	was, were	to go	went	to sit	sat
to bring	brought	to have	had	to speak	spoke
to buy	bought	to know	knew	to spend	spent
to come	came	to lose	lost	to stand	stood
to cost	cost	to make	made	to swim	swam
to cut	cut	to pay	paid	to take	took
to do	did	to put	put	to teach	taught
to draw	drew	to read	read	to think	thought
to drink	drank	to run	ran	to understand	understood
to eat	ate	to say	said	to wear	wore
to forget	forgot	to see	saw	to win	won
to give	gave	to sell	sold	to write	wrote

13 The verb *to be*

The verb **to be** is used to describe people, things and situations.

- Use the verb **to be** to talk about age.
  Jenny's little brother **is** five years old.
  Next year, I **will be** 13.

- Use the verb **to be** to talk about feelings.
  I**'m** hungry.
  She **was** thirsty after the race.
  We **will be** very happy.

THE SIMPLE PRESENT

Affirmative	Negative	Interrogative
• Note the contractions.	• Place **not** after the verb. • Note the contractions.	**Yes/no questions** • Invert the subject and verb.
I **am** I**'m** first. You **are** You**'re** next. She **is** She**'s** third. We **are** We**'re** fourth. They **are** They**'re** last.	I **am not** I**'m not** athletic. You **are not** You **aren't** patient. He **is not** He **isn't** nervous. We **are not** We **aren't** funny. They **are not** They **aren't** quiet.	**Am** I next? **Are** you ready? **Is** she absent? **Are** we on time? **Are** they finished? **Information questions** • Place the question word first. **Where** are you?

THE SIMPLE PAST

Affirmative	Negative	Interrogative
• There are no contractions. I **was** at your party. You **were** surprised. It **was** fun. Michael **was** in the kitchen. We **were** on the patio. They **were** in the pool.	• Place **not** after the verb. • Note the contractions. I **was not** I **wasn't** home. It **was not** It **wasn't** late. We **were not** We **weren't** cold.	**Yes/no questions** • Invert the subject and verb. **Were** you at home? **Was** Jenny at school? **Was** she the winner? **Were** they happy? **Information questions** • Place the question word first. **Where** were you?

THE FUTURE SIMPLE

Affirmative	Negative	Interrogative
• Use **will be** for all persons. • Note the contraction (**'ll**). I **will** I**'ll be** first in line. We **will** We**'ll be** there too.	• Use **will not be** for all persons. • Note the contraction (**won't**). I **will not** be ready. He **won't** be here. We **won't** be at the game.	**Yes/no questions** • Invert the subject and verb. **Will** he be 13 next year? **Information questions** • Place the question word first. **Where** will you be next year?

14 *Can*

We use **can** to talk about ability and permission.

A AFFIRMATIVE

• Use **can** with the <u>**base form**</u> of the verb.
> Jenny **can** <u>**think**</u> of good games for her little brother.
> Melissa **can** <u>**skate**</u> very fast.
> We **can** <u>**borrow**</u> two books from the library.

B NEGATIVE

• Use **cannot** with the <u>**base form**</u> of the verb. Note the contraction.
> We **cannot** <u>**run**</u> in the hall.
> I **can't** <u>**sing**</u> very well.

C INTERROGATIVE

Yes/no questions
• Invert the subject and **can**.
> **Can** Enrico play the guitar?
> **Can** you help me?
> **Can** we borrow your markers, please?

Information questions
• Place the question word first.
> **Who** can draw the pictures?
> **When** can you come?

15 The future simple

A AFFIRMATIVE

- Use **will** with the **base form** of the verb for all persons.
- The contraction is **'ll.**

I **will prepare** the menu.
You **will buy** the food.
They**'ll bring** the games.

B NEGATIVE

- Use **will not** for all persons.
- The contraction is **won't.**

I **will not** wash the dishes.
He **won't** clear the table.
We **won't** take the bus.

C INTERROGATIVE

Yes/no questions
Information questions

- Use **will** for all persons.
- Place the question word first.

Will he make a cake?
When will they arrive?

16 The imperative

The imperative (second person) is used to give instructions or orders.
- Use the **base form** of the verb without a subject.

Close the window.
Write your name on your sheet.
Cut out the pictures.
Help me, please.

The imperative (first person plural) is used to make suggestions.
- Use **let's** with the **base form** of the verb.

Let's look at the class yearbook.

STRATEGIES

Think as you learn...

1 **Plan your work.**

First, we collect pictures.

I agree. Next, we choose our favourites.

2 **Reflect on your progress.**

I know all these words. I can spell them too.

3 **Check your work.**

Oops! I think there are spelling mistakes.

I'll use a dictionary to correct my text.

4 Pay attention.

5 Use what you know.

6 Make a prediction.

7 Take a guess.

8 Practice.

9 Use resources.

10 **Take notes.**

11 **Look over the text.**

12 **Look for specific information.**

13 **Work together.**

14 **Take chances.**

15 **It's OK not to know everything.**

THE WRITING PROCESS

1 THINK

- Look at the model.
- Read the instructions.
- Think about what you will do.

2 ORGANIZE

- Assemble what you need.
- Take notes.
- Write down some ideas.

3 WRITE

- Prepare your first draft.
- Refer to the model and instructions.
- Ask for help if you have a problem.

4 REVISE

- Use the checklist.
- Ask a classmate to read your text.
- Make your corrections.

5 RECOPY

- Write the final copy.
- Use your best writing.
- Make sure you correct your mistakes.

6 SHARE

Suggestions
- Read your text to others.
- Make a class book.
- Record your text.